MERSEY

THE RIVER
THAT CHANGED
THE WORLD

MERSE

To Anthony H Wilson 1950-2007

© 2007

Published by The Bluecoat Press, Liverpool
Designed by March Graphic Design Studio, Liverpool
Map design by www.alexandermacgregor.co.uk
Printed by Grafo

Photography by Getty Image, Guy Huntington, Colin McPherson, Bill Meadows, National Musems Liverpool, Alan Novelli, Peel Holdings and Warrington Museum & Art Gallery (Warrington Borough Council).

ISBN 1 872568 55 5

The publisher would like to thank the many people who contributed to this book, including: Brian Alexander, Professor Peter Batey, Joe Dwek CBE, Professor Richard Evans, John Glester, Antony Gormley, Jude Habib, Janice Hayes of Warrington Museum, Mick Ord of Radio Merseyside, Dr Rob Philpott of National Museums Liverpool, Peter Walton, The Mersey People (Tom Workman, Kathleen Workman, Mary Kendrick MBE, Louise Clarke, Les Clarke, John Curry, Tony Brand, Shanthi Rasaratnam MBE, Dave Sandman, Dave Hall, Diane Walker, Sara Wilde, Paul Jelley, Simon Snodin, Alan Feast, Michael Heseltine, Chris Cleaver, Barney Easdown). Special thanks to Sharon King and Dan Walmsley at United Utilities and the team at Mersey Basin Campaign: Katie Bray, Neil Buttery, Kate Fox, Walter Menzies and Matthew Sutcliffe.

This book was published with financial assistance from United Utilities and initiated by the Mersey Basin Campaign.

MERSEY BASIN CAMPAIGN
WATERS I REGENERATION I ENVIRONMENT I SUSTAINABILITY

BBC RADIO MERSEYSIDE
95.8 FM & DAB Digital Radio

EY THE RIVER THAT CHANGED THE WORLD

EDITED BY IAN WRAY
COMMISSIONED PHOTOGRAPHY BY COLIN McPHERSON

THE BLUECOAT PRESS

CONTENTS

TIME AND THE RIVER IAN WRAY 8

BEFORE THE STORM EDWIN COLYER 14

THE NURSERY OF INNOVATION JOHN BELCHEM 20

ON THE WATERFRONT PETER DE FIGUEIREDO 28

MERSEY PEOPLE KATE FOX 46

CROSSINGS DEBORAH MULHEARN 80

WESTWARD HO! ANTHONY WILSON 94

DOWN TO THE SEA IN SHIPS MICHAEL TAYLOR 104

WILD MERSEY CHRIS BAINES 112

THE FLOW OF EVENTS PAUL UNGER 120

RIVER FUTURES STEVE CONNOR 130

ALONG THE BANKS DAVID WARD 138

MERSEY ROAD COLIN McPHERSON 146

CONTRIBUTORS 205

INDEX 206

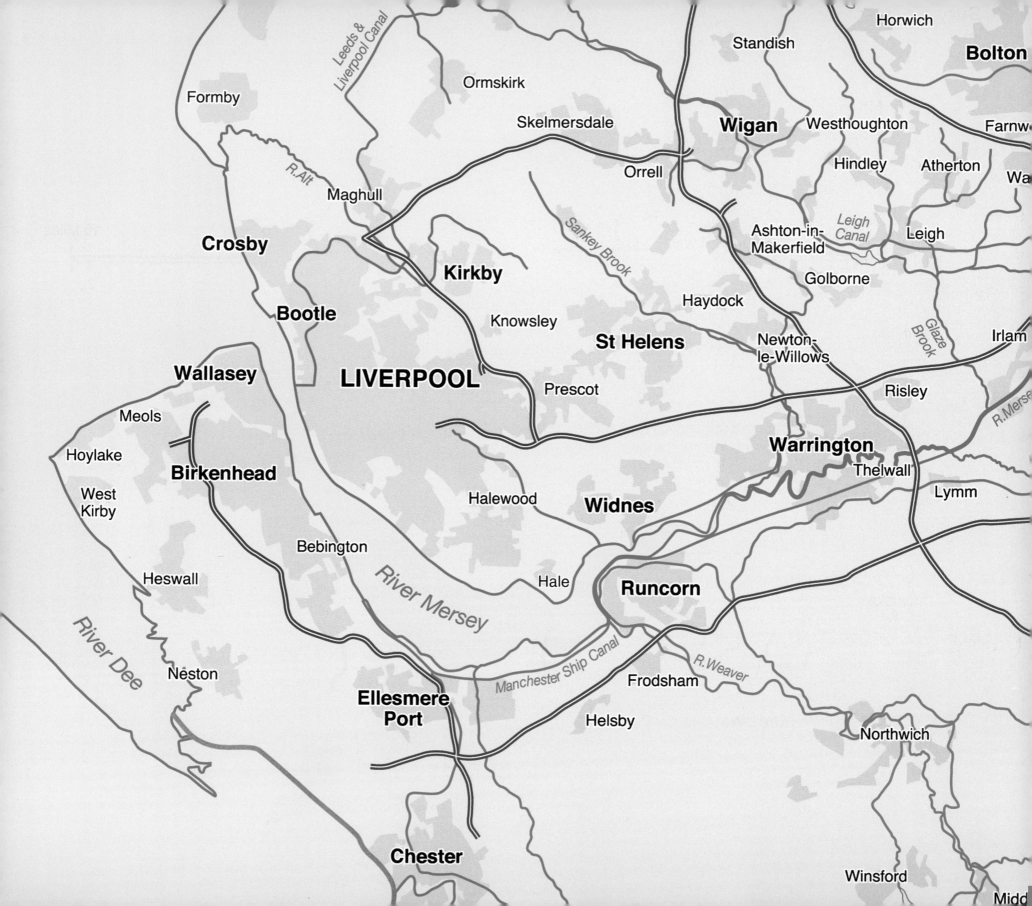

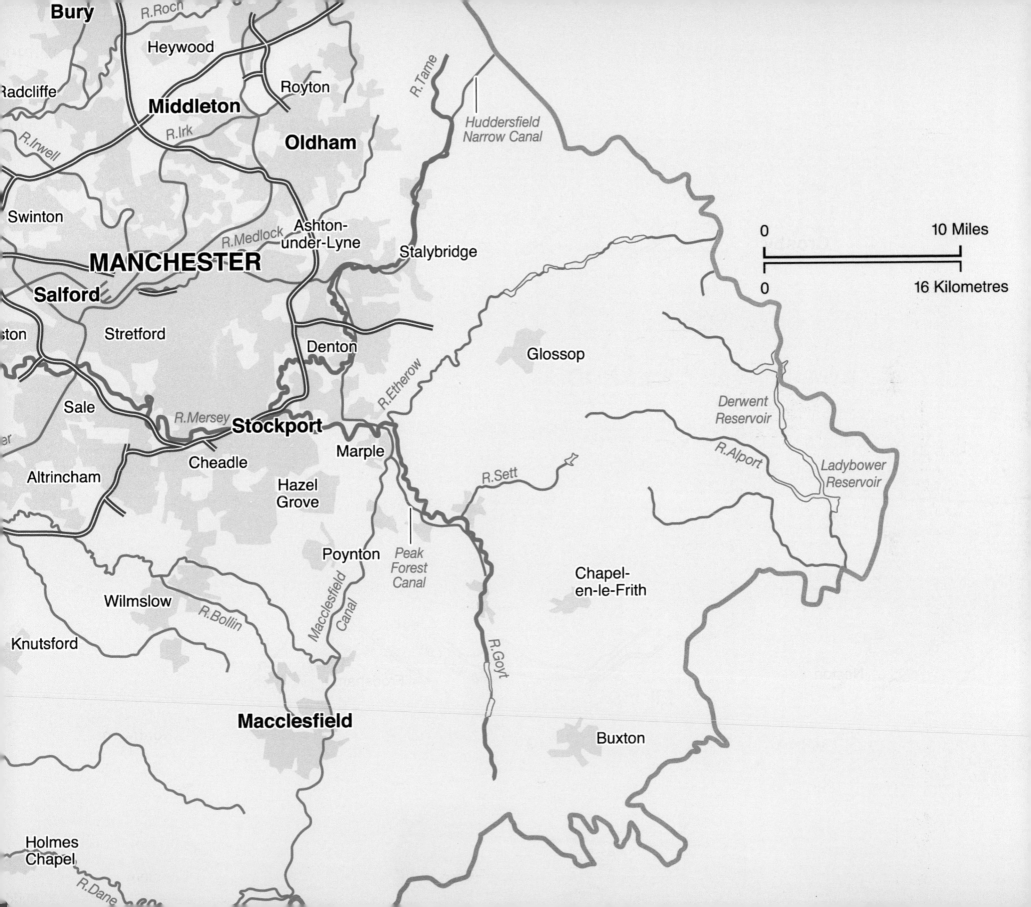

TIME AND THE RIVER

IAN WRAY

Opposite The mouth of the Mersey looking east towards Liverpool city centre. Royal Seaforth Dock is left foreground, facing New Brighton on the Wirral peninsula.

I am an estuary into the sea
I am a wave of the ocean
I am the sound of the sea
I am a powerful ox
I am a hawk on a cliff
I am a dewdrop in the sun
I am a plant of beauty
I am a boar for valour
I am a salmon in a pool
I am a lake in a plain
I am the strength of art

Amhairgain
Celtic Irish poet: possibly 4th century BC

It takes skill to moor a Mersey ferry at full tide. The trick is to approach the shore against the current and use the thrust from your engines – rather powerful engines in fact – to hold the ship parallel to the landing stage. Then heavy ropes are thrown, caught, coiled around capstans, and skilfully adjusted until the ship comes alongside the gangway.

This is a fast and powerful flow, and it is not a place for amateur sailors. Look at a map and you can see why. The Mersey is not just a large estuary, but a very unusual one. It is long – something like half of the total length of the river is estuarial, from Crosby through to Warrington – and the shape is odd too. Most estuaries are basically cone or funnel shaped, tapering from a wide mouth to a narrow river channel. The Mersey, unusually, has a very narrow section at its mouth, between Wallasey and Liverpool, where bluffs of harder Triassic rocks come down to the river, opening out to a much larger and wider estuarial basin beyond.

A powerful scouring action is set up in the constricted narrows by the repeated flushing of this huge basin. Silt and mud are constantly swept way, and the Mersey needs little dredging. Chester, once a port, sits at the head of the funnel shaped Dee estuary which has gradually silted up, putting an end to its maritime ambitions.

For obvious reasons the Mersey was no place for early mariners, dependant on paddles, hollowed out logs, or early sailing ships. So, until the late Middle Ages the river was a very powerful barrier to communications, not a conduit (Mersey is Old English for boundary river) and trade focussed on the lost port of Meols in Wirral, as Edwin Colyer recounts.

Before the railway builders bridged the Runcorn Gap in the 19th century, Warrington, at the head of the estuary, was the lowest bridging point. This was where the Roman Road to the north crossed the Mersey, and as John Belchem explains, Warrington's place on the river had some rather surprising and little known intellectual consequences.

From the 18th century onwards, the Mersey, and Liverpool, next to those scoured narrows, became the world's connection to a revolution in trade, industry and society — and shaped the first wave of what is now called globalisation. Manchester was the world's first industrial city and the Mersey its passage to the wider world in general, and the British Empire in particular. That fuse was lit by the construction of the first wet dock in the world in Liverpool in 1709.

Is it absurd to compare the Mersey with the Nile or the Albert Dock with the Pyramids of Giza? Perhaps it is. Yet the Pyramids are the remains of a dead civilisation which became a historical backwater. The industrial civilisation started on the Mersey's banks changed the world — and in China and India still does so today.

There was nothing kind, gentle or sustainable about the Mersey's rise to greatness. On the contrary, events were often driven by the most basic of human motives: conquest, personal gain, and self interest. In water, land and air, the natural environment was exploited and degraded, and is only beginning its long process of recovery.

Yet there are great legacies in the built environment. As Peter de Figueiredo explains, the physical artefacts, in docks, buildings and canals, are still with us. Like Stockport's striking railway viaduct and the Herculean Manchester Ship Canal, most are still everyday use. Liverpool's urban fabric has at last been recognised as a legacy of international significance, by the designation of parts of the city centre and former docks as a UNESCO World Heritage Site. These are some of the most varied and intact Victorian townscapes in the world.

We cannot avoid the truth. The slave trade was at the core of Liverpool's economy until its abolition in the 1807 (slavery was not abolished in the British colonies until 1833). The slavers wanted only personal profit and cared nothing for the black Africans who they forcibly exported to America. Yet unwittingly their cruel actions set in train huge cultural changes — including the emergence of black America with its distinct culture, leadership and music. As Anthony Wilson tells us, black music has shaped and defined popular culture, through the emergence of blues, rock and roll, soul, gospel, rock and jazz — the later arguably the

most important and original 20th century art form. Yet Wilson underplays the Mersey's hand. Rock and roll, created by Elvis Presley in Memphis, Tennessee, fused together the separate traditions of country music and the delta blues. And country music in turn has its origins in the culture of white settlers in the Appalachians, who had migrated to America from Scotland, Ulster and the north of England. They left Britain from the Mersey.

Perhaps the Mersey's days of greatness are over. Industry and empire may no longer be with us, and in some ways that is no bad thing. Nature is reclaiming the Mersey with a little help from the environmentalists, as Chris Baines says. Once abused and exploited, the Mersey is now recognised, especially by the European Union, as a nature conservation asset of international value, and a resource to be protected and nurtured.

The Mersey Basin as a whole is into the third decade of a massive clean up campaign, which, Paul Unger explains, has its origins in the actions of one entrepreneur turned political leader, Michael Heseltine, as well as the turbulent political events of the 1980s. So the salmon are back in the pool: yet the tide of events seems to have receded.

Or is that too easy an assumption? Certainly no one foresaw the cultural and musical flowering of the 1960s. When Daniel Defoe visited in 1708 he wisely avoided making predictions: "Liverpool is one of the wonders of Britain ... it still visibly increases both in wealth, people, business and building: what it may grow to in time I know not".

So often in the past the port connection has been the motor for greatness. Industry and empire always went hand in hand with maritime prosperity. It was the Cunard Yanks (stewards on the Cunard liners) who brought the black American recordings to Liverpool in the 1950s, again during an economic upswing in the port.

After a near eclipse in the 1980s, the port is on the up again, and as Michael Taylor says, handling even more trade than it did in the 1950s.

Opposite The Manchester Ship Canal with Runcorn Bridge in the background.

Above Situated at Salford Quays, on the bank of Manchester Ship Canal, The Imperial War Museum North designed by Daniel Libeskind is a symbol of our world torn apart by conflict.

11

Control has passed to a successful and entrepreneurial company, Peel Holdings (who incidentally recently disposed of a 49% share of the port business to the property investment arm of Deutsche Bank for around £750 million).

As if in harmony, Liverpool's city centre economy has taken off. In the last decade demand for office floor space has increased by over 200% (if present trends continue it could level peg with Manchester by 2011); since 1991 city centre living has increased by 500%; Grosvenor, the Duke of Westminster's property company, is on site with a £900 million project; and cranes festoon the skyline. Writer Simon Jenkins recently commented: "For lasting renewal, for a pattern of old and new responding rather than shouting at each other, for an urban personality in depth, I would look to newly emergent Liverpool".

Where Defoe sidestepped the future, Bill Gates, it could be argued, has devoted his life to anticipating and shaping it. As it happens, Bill has just invested $50 million in Liverpool – in the Liverpool School of Tropical Medicine to be precise – not as an act of charity for Liverpool, but because it is amongst the best in the world.

We are back again to geography and the river. The School of Tropical Medicine is another resonance from the British Empire and those Liverpool merchants. It was established in response to a call in 1898 from Joseph Chamberlain, British Colonial Secretary, for better trained doctors for the British colonies. Actually Chamberlain and his advisors wanted to train these colonial doctors exclusively in London (little changes). After something of a tussle, led by Liverpool merchant Alfred Lewis Jones, head of the Elder Dempster Shipping Line, the civil servants relented and allowed Liverpool to establish its own school as well. The School duly opened six months before its London equivalent.

Bill Gates is not investing for profit, of course, but as an act of philanthropy. His funding, from the Bill and Melinda Gates Foundation, will develop safer, more effective and longer lasting insecticides for mosquito control, and improved bed nets, and help to deploy the new insecticides and nets. As Bill points out: "Millions of children have died from malaria because they were not protected … if we can expand malaria control programs and invest what's needed in research and development we can stop this tragedy". So in a much gentler, kinder and humane way, the Mersey, and some of the people who live by it, may yet again change the world.

BEFORE THE STORM

EDWIN COLYER

To appreciate fully Merseyside's connection to the sea, pick a clear day, and explore the coast around Hoylake. The adventurous can walk out to Hilbre Island and admire the unfailing flux of the tides. The sands disappear, the waves cut you off; you are left on the exposed rocky outcrops until the tide retreats. If you are feeling fit, then climb to the top of Leasowe Lighthouse. From here it is easy to see the area's maritime heritage; tankers cut across the Irish Sea and Liverpool glitters on the opposite bank of the Mersey estuary.

For the less energetic, just take a stroll along the sea wall. Enjoy the breeze, watch the shrimpers and try to spot an oystercatcher probing the flats. But do not ignore the sea defences themselves, for the imposing concrete structures that line the coast have played a key role in a story that is only just coming to light: the sea wall has halted coastal erosion along the North Wirral coast, but it has also led to the destruction of one of Britain's most fascinating archaeological sites.

Locals on the Wirral know Meols (pronounced 'Mells' from the Norse for 'dunes') as more or less a suburb of Hoylake. But among archaeologists, this name means so much more. The discovery of vast numbers of archaeological finds and the evidence of dwellings and buildings in the sands around Dove Point suggest that this site was once a busy port and probably played an important role in trade and the economy of the Mersey region.

The first clues about the significance of Meols began to wash ashore in the 18th century. Expansion of the docks at Liverpool and dredging in the Mersey estuary changed the coastal dynamics of the region and altered the erosion patterns along the Wirral shore. As the sea began to eat away at the dunes, it uncovered a stash of ancient artefacts. From the late 18th century and through the 19th century locals regularly picked up trinkets – arrow heads, coins, brooches, buckles, jewellery – and all manner of other treasures from the sands at low tide.

The first earnest collector of these curios was a merchant from Liverpool, Mr P Ainslie. However, the archaeological significance of the finds was first recognised by Rev Abraham Hume, a typical Victorian antiquarian. During a visit to Hoylake parsonage in 1846 he noticed a small collection of finds gathered by Mrs Longueville, the parson's wife. In his book Ancient Meols of 1863, Hume recounts: "It appeared that these and numerous other metallic articles had been found by an old man of the village … [who] had amused himself at intervals with picking up curious piece of metal when the tide had retired. He did not attach much importance to them, and the best of them were given to children as toys." Hume gathered together as many of the items as he could borrow and, later in 1846, he gave the first formal exhibition of the finds. Ancient Meols had made made it into academia.

A number of other gentlemen historians and collectors quickly took an interest in the site, each amassing their own collection of finds. But it is Hume in the 1870s who first begins to wonder just what kind of a place Ancient Meols may have been. He is the first to rule out shipwrecks or the suggestion that the objects were carried down the Dee from Chester and deposited on the North Wirral shore. Instead he firmly believes that the finds have been uncovered from the remains of an abandoned settlement which used to be at Dove Point, and he notes the outlines and remains of old buildings that are visible in the sands at the lowest tides.

Speculation and discussion amongst this burgeoning population of 'modern' archaeologist was rife. But in the 1890s the local authorities built the first sea wall. The rapidly eroding coastline was saved, but Meols was lost: the sea wall once again changed the water currents and the secrets of this ancient settlement were washed out to sea. The Rev Hume and his generation of early archaeologists eventually died and Ancient Meols was all but lost – again.

The recent work of Dr David Griffiths from Oxford University and Dr Rob Philpott from Liverpool Museum is once again brings Meols back into the open. "I'd been looking at some of the finds from Meols in our collection over a period of 20 years," says Philpott, "and I was always struck that the site was probably very important. But as the finds are scattered in collections across the entire Northwest and beyond, it was difficult to know how to assess and analyse them properly. In 1999 we decided to collaborate and catalogue all the finds in detail as a starting point for their subsequent historical analysis."

Griffiths agrees that the complete cataloguing of the Meols finds was a critical starting point. "There was no particular point when Meols was discovered in the way that Tutankhamen's tomb was found by the glint of gold. The cataloguing was essential to bring Moels out of its latest period of obscurity and to discover how it fitted into the bigger picture of our heritage."

The cataloguing project was a formidable task, locating, identifying, describing and photographing more than 3000 objects. "One thing that this project did was to allay our fears that the Meols collections were not real," notes Philpott. "People have said that there are too many finds, too many exotic things. But our understanding of artefacts has caught up with Meols. Coins from pre-Roman Carthage and Celtic Brittany are certainly highly unusual, but not inexplicable."

Viewed in their entirety, the Meols finds provide a tangible chronology of the ancient site. The tree stumps in the Dove Point sands, along with the finds of Stone Age flints and Bronze Age pottery suggest that between ten and three thousand years ago this low lying coastal area would have been covered in dense forest. Our ancestors roamed the region, gathering berries and plants, catching wildfowl and fish on the plentiful coastal wetlands, and venturing into the forests for elk and wild boar.

Ancient Meols probably became settled permanently sometime between 500 and 0BC. The site was situated between the natural borders of the Dee and the Mersey and the political borders of three Celtic tribes – the Deceangeli of the North Wales coast, the Brigantes of Lancashire and Cumbia and the Cornovii of Cheshire and Staffordshire. Meols was perfectly placed for inter-tribal and international trade.

Along with the rustic ironware typical of this period, the Meols collections also contain coins from Carthage, Brittany and some very early Roman material possibly dating from before the conquest of Britain. "These apparently unusual items fit in with what we now know about Iron Age trade routes," explains Griffiths. "Meols was probably one of the stopovers for maritime traders following the western coast of Britain. It is the only identified Iron Age port in the Northwest. It was probably a major point in the region for regional and international maritime trade."

The Meols site has produced a rich variety of objects spanning the entire Roman period, too. The discovery of coins and military paraphernalia like belt buckles and brooches suggest that in its earliest Roman days Meols may have been a military outpost. However, the military presence soon appears to leave (favouring the 'bright lights' of the rapidly growing military town of Chester), yet Meols thrives. Roman material includes glass, pottery, and more than 70 brooches and 120 coins. Meols was a diverse and colourful port in an area that was otherwise economically underdeveloped. It was probably the place where the indigenous Britons continued to trade (and avoid the Roman taxes that would be levied in the port of Chester).

After the Romans, the Saxons and the Vikings continued to use Meols as a major port and trading post in the region. In particular, after the Vikings were ousted from Dublin in 902AD, a large number settled on the Wirral. The Mercian Queen Ethelfleda gave permission for the Norse leader Ingimund and his peoples to settle peacefully on the peninsular. The Wirral functioned as a semi-autonomous state, and even had its own parliament at Thingwall. As a port, Meols linked the Wirral Vikings to their scattered country folk, part of a trading network that included Dublin, York and Scandinavia.

But whilst the evidence suggests that Meols was an important port from its Iron Age beginnings through to the 10th century, the number of finds from this period are small compared to those from Medieval times (12th – 16th century). The variety and number of objects recovered from Meols for this period is second only to London, and far greater than the collections from well established medieval towns such as York or Bristol.

During this time Meols seems to enjoy modest prosperity. The finds from this period include a large quantity of personal effects, such as buckles, brooches and pilgrim badges from Rome, France and Canterbury. Crucibles and some unfinished items provide evidence of some local metalworking, suggesting that the settlement's permanent population has expanded. It is impossible to say how many people lived there at any time, notes Griffiths however. "It could have been as many as 30 or 40 households, perhaps, but always against a backdrop of seasonal activity with fairs and markets swelling numbers to many times this figure."

Then suddenly it all comes to an end; no objects have been retrieved from later than the early 16th century. Philpott thinks the end was probably catastrophic, and suggests the possibility of a dramatic sandstorm. "Climate change from warm to colder temperatures led to tremendous winds in the Atlantic around this time," Philpott explains. "Many of the finds were found under a preserving layer of sand. The rise of Liverpool across the Mersey and the encroaching sands were already leading to Meols' decline. Perhaps a storm even dumped a load of sand on Meols and buried the settlement overnight."

"What makes Meols remarkable today is the extraordinary chain of circumstances that have led to so much stuff being found," he continues. "Meols was exceptional in all stages. The sudden

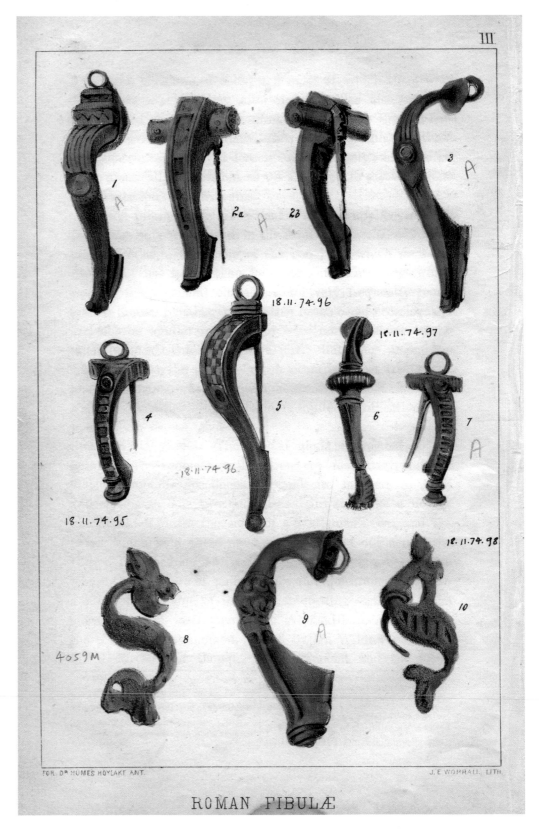

ROMAN FIBULÆ

abandonment of the settlement meant that more objects were left behind than if there had been a gradual decline. Then, buried under sand, more objects than normal were well preserved. Finally, more were found as the tidal erosion tended to pile the metal objects into hollows in the sands and people then went out looking for them. In terms of archaeology and the contribution Meols has made to our understanding of this region's past, this long-forgotten place is of the utmost importance.

"What is most remarkable about Meols is its long and continuous habitation of 2000 years. During this time it benefited from its geographical and political location between the Dee and Mersey. It has always been on the political peripheries, and its coastal location and protected anchorage made it the ideal site for maritime trading."

Philpott believes that as the Northwest's oldest port, Meols was probably more significant than documentary evidence (of which there is very little beyond the Domesday Book) would have us believe. Perhaps, he wonders, there are still more clues lying around. Perhaps they are buried beneath the dunes, or even under that imposing sea wall. "We have plans to go back into the field eventually," he says. "If there is still some settlement to find, perhaps Meols could become the most important archaeological dig in uncovering Merseyside's colourful past."

THE NURSERY OF INNOVATION

JOHN BELCHEM

At the tidal head of the River Mersey, Warrington has always benefited from its location. While not the first to discover the convenience of the river crossing, the Romans grasped the economic potential along the banks of the Mersey around what they called Veratinum, or 'ford town'. Archaeological remains testify to the manufacture of iron, bronze and pottery in the Roman station at Wilderspool. The first recorded bridges, initially somewhat flimsy wooden structures, date from the early 14th century, enhancing the flow of people and goods from across the region to Warrington's conveniently located fairs, markets and courts. Waterway developments from the 18th century brought further benefits. The Mersey-Irwell Navigation enabled river-born traffic to flow in both directions, not only downstream (through the tidal shallows between Warrington and Runcorn) to the great commercial seaport of Liverpool but also upstream (in flat-bottomed barges) to Manchester, arguably the world's first industrial city; the Weaver Navigation opened up the Cheshire salt fields; and the Bridgewater Canal, a mile and a half to the south of town, brought cheap coal and direct links to the whole system of inland navigation.

The lowest bridging point on the Mersey, Warrington was destined to become the main traffic node of the 'near north', the gateway to Lancashire. Long before the advent of the motorway network, Warrington was busy and congested, the natural intersection of the old highroad from London to Carlisle and Scotland and the crossroad from Chester to York. Where today's car-drivers sit impatiently in traffic snarl-ups, earlier generations of travellers took advantage of the town's famous inns, such as the Red Lion on Bridge Street, specially built to accommodate those whose business necessitated crossing the river Mersey.

Thanks to its prime river crossing location, Warrington generated a remarkable flow of people, goods and ideas, an ideal environment for innovation. The first town in Lancashire to introduce one of Bolton and Watt's steam engines, 18th century Warrington had all the right connections for economic growth, but historians have tended to overlook its pivotal role in the industrial revolution. A number of reasons account for this oversight (including perhaps the town's later translation from 'industrial' Lancashire into 'shire county' Cheshire). Precisely because of its waterway advantages, Warrington developed in multi-form manner as 'the town of many industries' (to quote a chapter title from Arthur Bennett's celebratory history written in 1900), without the kind of single industry specialism found elsewhere in the north. There were long-term economic benefits in such diversity, but this broad-based profile left industrial Warrington without a distinctive 'foundational' character and image to register in the historical record. Where other northern towns, as Stephen Caunce has shown, were highly specialized and proud of it, constructing their identity within a network of creative rivalry and economic complementarity, Warrington was everything and nothing, a bland blend cursed by ever increasing traffic congestion. Then there is the factor of size. Located midway between two major cities, Warrington has been overshadowed by Liverpool and Manchester. When the two cities were joined by the first railway line, Warrington was initially by-passed, reached only by a branch line, but the opening of the Grand Junction line from Crewe, and subsequently the arrival of the west coast main line, reaffirmed the town's nodal position. The development of the motorway network has confirmed the historical pattern: midway Warrington serves as natural distribution centre (and retail park) for its huge equidistant neighbours.

It is time for a more positive reassessment of the Mersey bridgehead. Early industrial Warrington, it is suggested here, offers an object lesson in

Opposite The magnificent Georgian Town Hall was originally built as a home for Thomas Patten in 1750. Designed by James Gibbs, the building was purchased by the town council in 1872 along with 13 acres of surrounding land. However, it is the Golden Gates that capture the most attention. Made for the International Exhibition of 1862, they were donated to the town by Frederick Monks and installed in 1895. Photograph Bill Meadows.

economic adaptability, technology transfer and the knowledge economy. The town was imbued with 'innovative essence', to use Peter Hall's terminology, that elusive but seemingly indispensable component of economic success which seems to flourish best at major intersections. Bridgehead of the river that changed the world, Warrington contributed much to the industrial revolution.

In the 18th century, Warrington was best known for the production of sail cloth, supplying 'half of the sail-cloth used in the navy', John Aikin recorded in 1795 in his Description of the Country from Thirty to Forty Miles Round Manchester. Some estimates put the number of local workers in the trade as high as 10,000. Always vulnerable to fluctuations in the state of foreign affairs, demand being highest at times of war, this 'staple' industry went into long-term decline after the end of the Napoleonic Wars. Its descent was subsequently hastened by the introduction of steam-powered vessels. With typical Warringtonian foresight, the leading firm of

Rylands Brothers abandoned sail-cloth production at the very beginning of the 19th century to move into the wire industry. By 1829 there were three wire works in the town as Warrington progressed quickly from traditional hand wire-drawing to the manufacture of the iron (later steel) winding cables essential to the exploitation of new deep mines in the adjacent Lancashire coalfield. Here Warrington made a crucial contribution to on-going industrialisation in the region.

As it advanced on a broad front, industrial Warrington itself never became a significant cotton town or primarily a chemical centre, despite favourable factors of economic geography in both instances. The local soap industry at Bank Quay, studied in immense depth by A.E. Musson in his monograph on Joseph Crosfield & Sons, exemplifies the kind of advantages offered by

Above The oldest known painting of Warrington shows the town from a house near Atherton's Quay. Painted by Thomas Donbavand in 1772.

Above The social and economic confidence of Warrington is expressed in this aquatint of a regatta on the Mersey in the 1840s.

Top Fishing for salmon in the Mersey at Warrington, c1790. Salmon was so common, it was a staple diet in the region's workhouses.

Above An 1840s engraving of the railway crossing the Mersey at Warrington with the industrial town in the background.

Top The original building which housed the Warrington Academy, 1757.

Photographs Warrington Museum & Art Gallery (Warrington Borough Council)

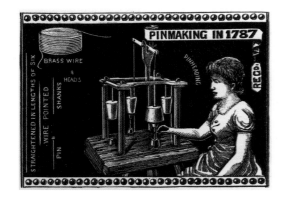

location in Warrington: tallow, palm oil, kelp and other imported raw materials could be brought cheaply by water from Liverpool, together with salt from Cheshire and coal from St Helens (essential ingredients for the Leblanc process of alkali production), while manufactured soap could be carried by river and canal to the populous inland towns and, via Liverpool, to expanding export markets. Alongside new manufacturing industry, Warrington retained a considerable (but typically not dominant) presence in the Lancashire metal trades, enjoying an enviable reputation for high quality production (an assessment which incidentally also applied to its malt, ales and brewing in general). The key figure here, the subject of a pioneer exercise in business history by T.S. Ashton, was Peter Stubs (1756-1806), the very personification of the diversity and ingenuity of the town's economic development. Tenant of the White Bear inn, Stubs combined the licensed trade with a successful file-making business (and the fathering of eighteen children). Dregs from beer barrels provided the basis of a paste which, once spread into the teeth of the files, gave them legendary durability and strength, a reputation cherished and maintained long after by the company he founded. 'To files may be added chisels, graving, watch and clock makers' tools, hand vices, pincers, metal and wire gauges, cutting pliers, and an extensive variety of articles', Dr Dionysius Lardner recorded in 1833: 'The

metropolis of this trade is Warrington, where, in the old-established manufactory of Stubs, every one of the numerous articles sold under the name of 'tools', in the common meaning of the term, is produced in a style of perfection not, probably, to be surpassed in the world. In this line even Birmingham yields the palm of superiority to Warrington.' Although they attracted an international market (and much counterfeiting), Stubs's files were sold primarily to machine workers in the adjacent industrial districts where, as the mechanical engineer James Nasmyth noted approvingly, 'every workman gloried in the possession and use of such durable tools'.

The archetypal self-made man, Richard Arkwright, a former barber turned 'inventor' of cotton-spinning machinery and cotton manufacturer, appreciated the value of Warringtonian technical expertise and gadgetry. Renowned for his guile in borrowing and exploiting the ideas (and capital) of others, Arkwright met and befriended a Warrington clockmaker John Kay (not to be confused with the John Kay who invented the flying shuttle) in a local public house. Encouraged by Arkwright over a glass or two of wine, Kay duly produced a model for a water frame or spinning by rollers, drawing upon work he had already undertaken for Thomas Highs of Leigh. Aided by other Warrington mechanics, Kay (who was soon indentured to Arkwright) spent the next few months developing the revolutionary machine, keeping the true

24

purpose secret by claiming they were 'making a Machine to find out the Longitude'. Having appropriated and patented the invention, Arkwright left Lancashire to establish factory-based spinning with the water frame in the remote location of Cromford near Matlock, and then at Belper. By combining technology and innovative production management, his true forte, Arkwright secured colossal productivity gains, but over time he was unable to protect his patents or overcome the handicaps of transport costs and isolation from further technical developments. As Arkwright discovered to his cost, new industry and new systems of production thrived best in the area where he had acquired his initial ideas, in the close juxtaposition of textile and engineering trades around Manchester. In this innovative milieu, there was a vibrant synergy driven in no small part by the skill and adaptability of mechanics engaged in the Warrington metal trades.

Warrington, however, provided much more than practical technological innovation and adaptability. Through its famous Dissenters' Academy it supplied the educational thrust for the industrial revolution. Opened in October 1757 mainly through the determined effort of the Rev John Seddon, minister of the Cairo Street Chapel, Warrington Academy was established by Lancashire nonconformists to provide higher education free from the Anglican religious tests imposed at Oxford and Cambridge, then infamous

for their intellectual torpor. By no means the first Dissenting Academy, Warrington represented the zenith of a movement dedicated, Sidney Pollard observed in his study of the industrial revolution and the genesis of modern management, to 'the great awakening of the human mind to scientific and humanist discovery'. Its small salaries notwithstanding, Warrington Academy acquired a highly talented array of tutors, attracted by its liberal reputation, including Joseph Priestley, William Enfield, John Aikin, George Walker and Gilbert Wakefield. Undeterred by its unprepossessing location, Mrs Barbauld,

Warrington, the 'town of many industries'. Imported raw materials could be brought cheaply by water from Liverpool, salt from Cheshire, coal from St Helens while manufactured goods could be carried back by river, canal and, later rail to the expanding markets worldwide. The town developed a diversity of industries: **Opposite from left** pinmaking (where the advertising boasted their fine quality was due to the nimble fingers of child labour; soap making (with Joseph Crosfield taking advantage of Warrington's location to import tallow, palm oil and other ingredients from Liverpool); tool-making, where Peter Stubs built up an international reputation for its quality tools; and glass-making, tanning, wire-drawing amongst many other trades at which the town excelled. **Above** Carton makers; packing Crosfield soaps; wire manufacturing, a major industry from which Warrington Rugby League team gets its nickname of 'The Wires'.
Photographs Warrington Museum & Art Gallery (Warrington Borough Council)

Right Although Warrington was not ideally placed, it built up a reputation for shipbuilding in the early 19th century. It reached its zenith with the building of RMS Tayleur. When launched sideways into the Mersey at Warrington in October 1853, Tayleur was the largest merchant ship on the seas. Chartered by the White Star Line to serve the booming Australian trade routes, Tayleur left Liverpool on 19 January 1854, on her maiden voyage to Australia.

Unfortunately, the ship's compasses were not correctly set to account for her iron hull. The crew believed that they were sailing south through the Irish Sea, but were actually travelling west towards Ireland. In stormy seas, on 21 January 1854, the ship was heading straight for land. Despite dropping both anchors as soon as rocks were sighted, she ran aground on the east coast of Lambay Island, about five miles from Dublin Bay.

Attempts were made to lower the ship's lifeboats, but when the first one was smashed on the rocks, launching further boats was deemed unsafe. Tayleur was so close to land that the crew was able to collapse a mast onto the shore, and some people aboard were able to clamber along it to land. Out of the 652 people onboard, 380 lives were lost. The White Star connection has drawn comparisons with the Titanic disaster over 50 years later. For Warrington, the tragedy was to mark the end of its shipbuilding industry.

Photographs Warrington Museum & Art Gallery (Warrington Borough Council)

née Aikin, daughter of one of the tutors, looked to the Academy to fulfil the highest goals, training the next generation of the nation's leaders:

> Mark where its simple front yon mansion rears,
> The nursery of men for future years:
> Here callow chiefs and embryo statesmen lie,
> And unfledg'd poets short excursions try:
> While Mersey's gentle current, which too long
> By fame neglected, and unknown to song,
> Between his rushy banks, (no poet's theme)
> Had crept inglorious, like a vulgar stream,
> Reflects th' ascending seats with conscious pride,
> And dares to emulate a classic tide

Looking back from the 19th century, the Academy – which lasted a bare thirty years – was doubtless accorded inflated importance by local antiquarians who delighted in portraying Warrington as 'the Athens of the north'. In this invocation, the Academy was the coping stone of a remarkable local cultural infrastructure embracing William Eyres' printing press, apparently without equal in Lancashire, and the Warrington Circulating Library, forerunner of municipal public libraries. A publishing outlet for the tutors who 'maintained an academic atmosphere and created a distinct literature in a manner that was unrivalled, except at a university', Eyres' press published some 200

works between 1760 and 1802 as well as Eyres' Weekly Journal; or the Warrington Advertiser, the second oldest newspaper in Lancashire. A cultural facilitator, Eyres also served as the first librarian of the Circulating Library established in 1760, a resource patronised by the Academy tutors. Its fine collection of books ultimately served as the nucleus of the Warrington Municipal Library established under the Museums Act of 1845, the first library in the country supported by local rates.

In retrospect the Academy represents something far more than a nonconformist substitute for Oxbridge on the banks of the Mersey. Regarded by some commentators as the first 'redbrick' university, the model for universities and university colleges throughout 'civic' Britain, Warrington Academy is perhaps better described as the first Polytechnic. This designation, suggested by Peter Hall, captures the spirit and mission of the Academy, a crucial catalyst in inspiring an innovative industrial milieu. Much to the approval of its sponsoring nonconformist industrialists, there was a distinctly vocational emphasis with modern subjects taking precedence over traditional training for the learned professions: perhaps 200 of the 393 students, it has been calculated, went into commerce and industry. Appointed to tutorship in languages and belles-lettres, Joseph Priestley, discoverer of oxygen, played a key role in redesigning the curriculum, abandoning the standard course of studies designed for students entering the learned professions. The

progressive attitudes of the tutors can be seen in William Enfield's Essay towards the history of Leverpool, published and printed by Eyres in 1773, which took unashamed delight in the progress of commerce and trade, factors which outweighed the lack of a venerable past: 'The history of a place which has lately emerged from obscurity, and which owes, if not its being, at least its consequence to the commercial and enterprizing spirit of modern times, cannot be supposed to afford many materials for the entertainment of the curious antiquarian.'

After a series of personal, religious, political and financial controversies, problems apparently compounded by indiscipline among the students, the Warrington Academy was suspended in 1783 and dissolved in 1786 by which time the initiative had passed to the New College of Arts and Sciences in Manchester. From the outset, the Manchester Academy was a 'mechanic school' with an exhibition, a laboratory and a commitment to 'mechanick arts'. Once again, Warrington had shown the way for others to follow and develop.

At celebrations to mark the bicentenary in 1957 of the founding of the Academy, Dr Bronowski drew attention to two fundamental ways in which the Warrington Academy had contributed to economic growth and progress:

They were the men, they and their students, and their students in turn, who made the Industrial Revolution, and they did not make it by mechanical skill but because they learned here an intellectual approach which baulked at nothing and looked upon everything afresh. It was this intellectual attitude which made the Industrial Revolution possible and which made it great. Secondly, it was made possible because these people formed a kind of education which was quite unique. They broke the old spell of vocational education which was mainly designed for men who were entering the theological or medical professions.

Bridgehead of the Mersey, early industrial Warrington was never 'the Athens of the north', but given the remarkable flow of people, goods and ideas across and along the river and associated waterways, it was well placed to challenge old ways and to generate new approaches and attitudes. Although no longer the lowest bridging point, Warrington has continued to prosper from its prime location, the logistical hub of the industrial and urban north west. Always overshadowed by its big city neighbours on either side, Warrington has not been accorded the recognition it deserves. Straddling the Mersey, it was of critical importance in the initial matrix of industrialization, a true pioneer in technical innovation, knowledge transfer and the knowledge economy.

Above Bishop's Wharf, Warrington. By the end of the 19th century, the town had become a major industrial centre with its accompanying problems of pollution. The Mersey still played its part as the photograph shows but the photograph of the bridge (right) shows dredging taking place to keep the waterways open from the increasing problems of silt.

ON THE WATERFRONT

PETER DE FIGUEIREDO

Opposite The Ineos chemical plant at Weston Point, Runcorn. Of Runcorn's former industries, all but the chemical industry have disappeared. The industry dominated for many years by ICI has since been taken over by Ineos.
Photograph by Alan Novelli

The Mersey waterfront is a product of the industrial revolution. Over the past 300 years, the riverside scene has been transformed. For the early 18th century traveller journeying down the River Mersey, the impression would have been largely rural. Some buildings would have been glimpsed, perhaps a scattering of cottages and farms, the odd medieval church or timber-framed manor house. In the small towns of Stockport and Warrington, workshops and dwellings huddled together on the river banks, whilst at Liverpool, still a modest port, warehouses, hostelries and lodging houses clustered around the pool. Apart from the ruined castle at Halton and the remains of the priory at Birkenhead, there was no architecture of any great ambition. 100 years later, industrialisation had taken hold, and over the following century urban expansion occurred on an unprecedented scale.

From the port of Liverpool, with its great docks and warehouses, and its links to international markets, the region's products of industrialisation were despatched around the globe. Yet the earliest factory goods were produced not on the Mersey itself, but along its minor tributaries in east Lancashire and north-east Cheshire, where silk, cotton and woollen mills, powered by water, were built. Few of these buildings survive, but Quarry Bank Mill of 1784 on the banks of the Bollin at Styal, and the much smaller wool scribbling mill of 1779 on the River Tame at Delph, are typical of the early industrial period in their simple proportions and functional design.

The Tame and the Goyt, the tributaries where our present day journey begins, feed into the Mersey at Stockport, a medieval market town that was radically altered by the industrial revolution. The old town occupied the valley bottom together with the steep slopes leading up to the market place and to the medieval church, where the tumble of roofs and dizzying drops in level are best seen from the iron bridge that crosses Little Underbank and from the great railway viaduct with its giant brick arches that stride across the valley high above water level. Yet the river which gave form to this distinctive topography is neglected. In the 1930s the Mersey was covered over with a roadway, which later

29

Right The M60 motorway passing under
Stockport viaduct with, lit up in the background,
the Pyramid office development.
Photograph by Alan Novelli

became the pedestrian thoroughfare of a vast and featureless shopping centre, its present dismal state
a legacy of misplaced utopian ideas. In recent years, however, attention has returned to the old
marketplace and the surrounding network of narrow streets, where the Council's current policy of
conservation and renewal has re-established local pride in the old town. The exemplary restoration of
the half-timbered 17th century Staircase House as a visitor centre has provided a historic focus.

The river valley at Stockport is also now the course of the M60 motorway, and just west of the
town centre between motorway and river is another piece of utopianism, the Pyramid Office Building.
This crystal of blue glass built in 1992, set in a desolate landscape of road junctions and
roundabouts, has provided the local name for the area – 'the Valley of the Kings'.

Down river from Stockport and the spirit of ancient Egypt the Mersey meanders through a wide
flood plain that bisects the southern suburbs of Manchester. The towers of several medieval churches
can be seen from the river marking the old villages that have been swallowed up by suburban sprawl.
At Cheadle, Didsbury, Northenden and Flixton are churches that serve as focal points for their
communities, even if they no longer stand amongst green fields. But they are often upstaged by
Victorian churches erected at the expense of Manchester bankers, mill owners and traders, who built
their houses on the outer fringes of the city. Sir James Watts, a classic Manchester self-made
businessman and proprietor of what was then the largest drapery business in the world, built a
spectacular Gothic house, Abney Hall which stands overlooking the river at Cheadle. The house was
fitted out by the Roman Catholic architect Augustus Welby Pugin, but Watts himself was a dissenter,
and for the local community he built the nearby Congregationalist church in Mersey Road.

Most inspiring of all the churches that were built on the southern edge of the city is the Roman
Catholic church of All Saints at Barton-upon-Irwell, completed in 1868 and intended as a family
mausoleum for the de Trafford family. It is the masterpiece of Edward Welby Pugin, the son of
Augustus, and grew from being a mortuary chapel to a parish church and Franciscan Friary.
Immensely tall, with steeply pitched roofs, it soars above the desolate wasteland on the western edge
of Trafford Park. At the time the church was built, Trafford Park was a country estate, but the palatial
mansion house of the de Traffords was demolished when the Manchester Ship Canal arrived in 1894,
and the grounds became the world's first industrial estate, a potent symbol of economic progress.
Also seen from the Irwell, and more distantly from the Mersey, the domes and pasteboard glamour of
the Trafford Centre represent the consumerist symbol of modern times.

The original Trafford Park was an aristocratic family seat that found itself too close to the fast-encroaching city to survive. Many of the merchant villas that were built along this stretch of the Mersey in the Victorian period, however, remain. The Towers at Didsbury, designed by Thomas Worthington, is one of the grandest: it was built for John Edward Taylor, proprietor of the Manchester Guardian in 1872. At Rose Hill, Northenden, lived Sir Edward Watkin, the railway entrepreneur and proprietor of the Cheshire Lines railway, the tracks of which ran alongside his boundary wall. Two ancient houses also miraculously survive in Chorlton-cum-Hardy. Barlow Hall, a timber-framed courtyard house dating from the 1570s is now a golf clubhouse; whilst Hough End Hall, an E plan house built 20 years later for Nicholas Mosley, a Manchester cloth merchant who became Mayor of London and developed metropolitan taste, was much more up-to-date. A national preservation campaign in the 1920s prevented its demolition, but intensive development within the grounds has now ruined its setting.

At Irlam, the Mersey gushes over a foaming weir into the Manchester Ship Canal. The rubble of demolished factories and steel works is now colonised by wildlife, and continuing beyond the oil tanks of Cadishead and Partington, the scene becomes surprisingly rural. At Warburton, Old St Werburgh's Church is a charming mishmash of different styles and periods. Part timber framed, part stone and part 18th century brick, with an interior fitted out in the Jacobean period, it lost its role as the parish church in 1885 when a new place of worship was erected nearby. The rural idyll however is soon shattered by the massive concrete ramps of the Thelwall Viaduct which carry the M6 motorway over the canal. Beyond lies Warrington, a town that is older and more interesting than first appears.

Until the 20th century, Warrington was the lowest bridging point, and this gave it great strategic importance. Here the Romans crossed the river en route from Chester to Wigan, and established metal working, enamelling and ceramics industries. An important market town in the Middle Ages, it expanded in the early 18th century with the coming of the waterways, and the many turnpike roads that converge on the town bridge. The town's most striking landmark is the parish church of St Elphin, for its spire is the third tallest in Britain. Although the chancel is medieval, the remainder is Victorian, built for the Revd William Quekett, whose motto, according to local tradition, was 'always to a-spire'. The church stands oddly isolated from the town centre, for the river crossing was moved half a mile down stream not long after the church was built, thus causing the centre of gravity to shift away. The present reinforced concrete bridge of 1915 is the sixth on the site, but more unusual is the Bank Quay steel transporter bridge, which was built in the same year to carry goods across the Mersey to the former soap works of Joseph Crosfield & Sons. This bridge, a scheduled ancient monument, was last used in 1964 and needs urgent repair if it is to survive as one of only three such bridges in Britain and seven in the world.

Three miles down river from Warrington is Fiddler's Ferry, formerly a ferry crossing point, and then a river boat yard in the 19th century. Now it is the site of a huge coal-fired power station, built here for its proximity to the coal fields of St Helens. In the bright light of a cold autumn morning, clouds of vapour issue from the rims of the eight vast concrete cooling towers and drift out across the featureless flat landscape. On the other side of the river the ground rises to a rocky hilltop which is crowned by the ruins of Halton Castle, built for defence in the 12th century, and later owned by John of Gaunt, who used it as a hunting lodge. Clustered at the foot of the castle is a group of interesting buildings including a private library, built in 1733 by Sir John Chesshyre, prime sergeant to George II, the Castle Hotel, originally the 18th century courthouse of the Duchy of Lancaster, and the Seneschal's House of 1598. The Castle was garrisoned by the Royalists during the Civil War, then pulled down by the Parliamentarians. Later, it was adapted as an eyecatcher by Sir Richard Brooke to improve the view from his nearby house Norton Priory.

Right The Silver Jubilee Bridge is a compression arch suspended-deck bridge built in 1961 between Runcorn and Widnes. Designed by Mott, Hay and Anderson and built by Dorman Long, the original construction was a two lane road traffic bridge later increased to four lanes. Ferry crossings have been recorded at this spot as early as the 12th century.
Photograph by Alan Novelli

Norton Priory was originally founded in 1133 for Augustinian canons in a remote riverside location. The Brookes family acquired it at the Dissolution, and rebuilt it as a country house, retaining only the undercroft of the abbot's quarters. During the later 18th century the family opposed the encroachment of canals across their land, and then fought against railways and chemical fumes. Finally in 1928 they gave up the struggle, leaving the house to be demolished and the stone used to build a sulphuric acid plant. Today the site of the priory is an archaeological museum and a monastic garden, its great treasure being an 11 foot high medieval statue of St Christopher, formerly a devotional object for travellers fording the Mersey at low tide.

It was the misfortune of the Brookes of Norton Priory to live close to what became an industrial hot spot, for the twin towns of Runcorn and Widnes are now renowned for their toxicity and pollution. But initially it was the coming of the canals and the establishment of a transhipment point on the Mersey at Runcorn that led to the rapid development of the area. The first to see the potential was the Earl of Bridgewater, whose canal gave access to Manchester and its hinterland. In order that he could personally supervise the development of the wharfs and canal basin, he built himself an imposing mansion overlooking the construction site on the river bank (the house has recently been converted to flats). The Bridgewater Canal was followed by the Trent and Mersey Canal, which opened links with the Cheshire saltworks and the potteries. From the northern shore of the river, the Sankey Canal connected Widnes with the coal fields and glass making industries of St Helens. At Runcorn itself, red sandstone of excellent quality was quarried and transported down river for the construction of many of Liverpool's great Georgian and Victorian buildings. But the major economic expansion came with the establishment of the chemical industry, and in particular with the production of alkali, on which the manufacture of soap, glass and many Victorian household products depended.

Alkali production involves mixing salt with sulphuric acid, then burning it in a furnace with lime and coal, and Runcorn and Widnes were situated close to the sources of all the commodities required in that process. But the chemical factories threw vast quantities of hydrochloric acid gas and choking fumes into the atmosphere, damaging the health of the workers and local residents, whilst the toxic waste product (known as galligoo from the

oozing noise it made) found its way into the Mersey, producing hydrogen sulphide, characterised by its stench of rotten eggs. The nucleus of this unpleasant activity was Spike Island, the area of land bounded by the north bank of the river and the Sankey Canal. Today this is a nature reserve, with little trace of its industrial past, but the life of the workers is powerfully evoked at Catalyst, the nearby museum of the chemical industry that is housed in part of Hutchinson's former alkali works.

The river estuary at the Runcorn Gap is now dominated by the vast latticed steel arch of the road bridge and the tangle of elevated roadways that lead to it. Within this traffic-laden environment, a civilised waterfront environment has not yet emerged. This is in part because financial resources have been concentrated on Runcorn New Town to the exclusion of the old settlement at Runcorn, but also because the new housing built on the river frontage in recent years has failed to achieve a distinctive character. More successful is the Brindley Centre, a striking new theatre and gallery on the edge of the Bridgewater Canal, designed by John Miller and Partners, that has given Runcorn a lively cultural focus. Across the river at Widnes, which was described in 1888 by the Daily News as 'the dirtiest, ugliest and most depressing town in England', waterfront regeneration has scarcely begun.

From the Runcorn Gap, the estuary widens in a great sweep alongside the Weston Point Dock with its church built for the spiritual guidance of the watermen, past the salt works, the chemical plant and the power station on the hillside above, brightly illuminated at night by a firmament of shimmering lights, and on across the Frodsham Marshes to the ridge of hills beyond. The north bank is entirely rural, its outline punctuated only by the lighthouse at Hale Point which guided river boats past the treacherous sandbanks close to the shore. Nearby is a curiosity, a duck decoy dating from the early 18th century, and possibly earlier. Constructed in a marshy area, it consists of a moated enclosure with a hexagonal pool from which a series of tapering channels or 'pipes' leads off. At the end of the pipes were nets into which the ducks were driven by dogs. It is said that up to 1,500 ducks were trapped in a season, and though no longer in use, it is preserved as a rare example of wildfowling tradition. Just inland from the lighthouse is the village of Hale, which remains untouched by the industrial revolution. Clustered around the village green are the ancient church, groups of thatched whitewashed cottages, and the Manor House, originally the parsonage, with its elaborate Baroque frontage, added by the Revd. William Langford in the early 18th century.

On the south bank of the river, beyond the Frodsham marshes the smells take hold again, borne on the wind from the vast petro-chemical conglomeration at Stanlow, Thornton and Ince. This dramatic and sculptural landscape of fuel tanks and smoking chimneys, gantries and elevated walkways, all connected by miles of snaking metal pipes and cables grew up after the arrival of the Manchester Ship Canal, which runs alongside the river from Runcorn down to Eastham. But it is worth exploring the accessible parts of the area, not just for its wildlife, but for architectural treasures too. Ince Manor is a monastic grange built in the 13th century for the Benedictine Abbey at Chester (now the Cathedral). It has recently been rescued from dereliction by the Chester Buildings Preservation Trust. Stanlow Abbey, a late 12th century Cistercian Monastery where Edward I once stayed, is now part of a farm complex, and is quietly crumbling away. The medieval church at Thornton-le-Moors too needs rescuing, for it has recently been abandoned by its diminishing local community.

The town of Ellesmere Port beyond also profited from the coming of the Manchester Ship Canal, though industrialisation had already taken hold following the construction of the Ellesmere Canal (later the Shropshire Union) in 1796. Thomas Telford was the engineer, and he designed a series of magnificent docks and warehouses that were constructed between 1830 and 1843 on the banks of the river. These now house the National Waterways Museum, with a collection of objects related to canal heritage. In addition to the goods warehouses, the canal offices, engine houses and stables, there is a terrace of dock workers' cottages that survives from the same period. But Ellesmere Port has always had an image problem: in 1847 William Mortimer commented that "there is no town in the Kingdom, possessed of equal advantages, which presents so dull, – so gloomy an appearance". Today it still suffers, and even its showpiece, Telford's canal basin, is blighted by a group of recent apartment blocks that mimic, but fail woefully to capture the character of the Georgian structures they adjoin.

The Manchester Ship Canal terminates at Eastham just north of Ellesmere Port. Here the oil tankers discharge the crude oil that continues by pipeline to the refineries at Stanlow, and here also are engineering, papermaking and chemical factories. But the biggest employer in this area is Vauxhall Motors, which opened a car plant on the bank of the Mersey in 1963. Vauxhalls were persuaded to come to Ellesmere Port, an area of high unemployment, by government incentives, but they were also attracted by the site of Hooton Park This was the former country estate of Richard Naylor, a banker and property speculator, and one of the wealthiest businessmen in Victorian Liverpool. Hooton Hall boasted a tall tower and a columned sculpture gallery, and within the grounds there was a racecourse. But at the outbreak of the First World War, the Park was requisitioned, the Hall demolished and an aerodrome was created for the Royal Flying Corps, complete with a trio of aircraft hangars, their roofs constructed from flimsy Belfast trusses. Intended only for the duration of hostilities, the hangars, came into service again during the Second World War and still survive today, kept alive by a group of historic aircraft enthusiasts. In 1930 Hooton Park became the first civic airfield in the north of England, but three years later it was replaced by the new airport across the river at Speke.

The 1930s development of Speke was an ambitious municipal enterprise. It followed the acquisition of 730 hectares of the old Speke Hall estate to create a new industrial area to rival Trafford Park and to attract new industries to Liverpool. A boulevard runs parallel with the river, to the north of which the original industrial buildings were erected, whilst on the south side a new residential suburb grew up. By 1955 the population had reached 21,000, but more recently it has dramatically declined. To counter this, efforts have been made to regenerate the area, the focus being the rapid expansion of Liverpool John Lennon Airport. With the relocation of the airfield to a nearby site, the original Art Deco airport structures have been successfully adapted as a hotel, offices and leisure centre, the focus of the new Estuary Business Park. Less fortunate has been fate of Speke Hall, the beautiful 16th century moated house belonging to the National Trust, which has lost its once peaceful rural setting on the banks of the river, and is now blighted by the roar of aircraft. Yet it is an unexpected pleasure to find such a picturesque timber framed structure so close to a great city.

Continuing northwards from Speke, on both sides of the river the waterfront scene becomes more varied. At Garston are the cranes of a still active port, and beyond are the delightful marine residential estates of Cressington, Grassendale and Fulwood Park, laid out in the mid 19th century with stuccoed villas for prosperous Liverpool merchants. On the Wirral side too there are planned estates, such as Rock Park, where the large houses have fine river views. But more remarkable are the model villages built at Bromborough Pool and Port Sunlight for industrial workers rather than the business class who could afford a favoured location. Bromborough Pool is one of the earliest model villages in the country, created by Price's Candle Company for its factory workers in 1853. Alongside the factory, there are terraced houses, a church, school and village hall, together with a cricket ground and allotments. After the candle factory closed, the village declined; but recently it has been rescued by Riverside Housing Association, which is now fighting Wirral Council's decision to close the school on economic grounds. Much more

ambitious was Port Sunlight, the enlightened creation of W.H. Lever, First Viscount Leverhulme. Lever was one of the most successful businessmen of the Victorian age, and his money came from soap. He moved his factory from Warrington to the banks of the Mersey in 1888, with the idea of establishing an industrial village, where he combined his passionate interests in social improvement, architecture and landscape design. His village is the ultimate garden settlement, with avenues, walks, vistas, abundant greenery, statuary and monuments. The cottages, designed in many different styles, are grouped into blocks, neat and ordered as Lever favoured. For the recreation and improvement of his workforce he provided clubs and dining rooms, theatre and institute, schools and social facilities. At the centre of the village is the gallery built in memory of his wife that contains his astonishing art collection.

In his social mission, Lever was untypical of his class, but as a businessman he was bold, determined and ruthless. An establishment outsider, a non-conformist and an innovator, he embodied those virtues that led to and sustained the great seaport of Liverpool during its period of prosperity in the 18th, 19th and early 20th centuries. Today Liverpool is a World Heritage Site, inscribed as "the supreme example of a commercial port at the time of Britain's greatest global influence". The legacy of that imperial age is strikingly visible along the riverfront: in the urban landscape of the maritime city with its seven miles of docks, its dockside warehouses, its banks, offices and exchanges, in its cathedrals that crown the escarpment, and in the great cultural and civic buildings with their collections and works of art, in the public sculptures, and in the human endeavour that underpinned that relentless drive for profit, prosperity and civic achievement. Whilst the culture and the way of life of a great port no longer survives, the city's maritime connections with civilisations from across the globe have left a cosmopolitan outlook and enriched the flow of ideas and influence.

It is in Liverpool that the River Mersey reaches its architectural climax. Right on the river edge is the Albert Dock with its vast complex of bonded warehouses constructed in brick and cast iron, an engineering masterpiece that is unmatched in Europe. Opened in 1846, it was the work of Jesse Hartley, Liverpool's innovative dock engineer. Its successful conversion and reuse as museums and restaurants, shops and offices was the flagship of Liverpool's first phase of regeneration following Michael Heseltine's political intervention in 1981. Hartley's equally robust Stanley Dock warehouses, a mile further down river, however, remain empty, together with the gargantuan Tobacco Warehouse which towers over the central docks.

At the heart of the city is the Pier Head, a vast waterfront space created at the beginning of the 20th century as a transport hub, and full of activity when the Mersey was busy with passenger liners, merchant ships and cross river ferry boats. The Three Graces, as they have come to be known, which date from this period, are the symbol of Liverpool, memorable by their scale, confident swagger, and in the case of the Royal Liver Building, by its idiosyncratic outline of twin towers topped by the city's famous liver birds with their wings outstretched. Today, the city's changing skyline is a subject of vigorous debate amongst developers, city planners and conservationists. For whilst most World Heritage Sites consist of groups of static monuments where scope for change is strictly limited, Liverpool's redundant dockland and war-damaged hinterland is rapidly being developed as a new spirit of confidence and enterprise grips the city. A cluster of tall towers is appearing to the north of the Pier Head, a vibrant retail quarter is taking shape east of the Albert Dock, whilst a new waterfront performance arena adjoins it to the south. The scale, ambition and quality of this regeneration activity far surpasses the timid development schemes of the 1980s and 90s, and promises a sustainable future for the city that is European Capital of Culture in 2008.

Liverpool enjoys one of the most impressive settings of all English cities, and the finest views are to be had from the opposite banks of the river. But

Liverpool waterfront is one of the most recognizable city panoramas in the world. Dominated by the 'Three Graces' (the Royal Liver, Cunard and Port of Liverpool buildings), the historic waterfront has been granted World Heritage Site status.

Photograph by Alan Novelli

the Wirral waterfront has so far failed to benefit from its scenic potential. Whilst Liverpool's buildings, old and new, look outwards in celebration of the city's global connections, Birkenhead has turned its back on the river, hiding its architectural riches from view. Its only real landmark is the ventilation shaft for the Mersey Tunnel, massive and windowless, its outline of diminishing planes enlivened by syncopated patterns of canted bricks. But if the river prospect of Birkenhead fails to impress today, it is not for lack of ambition for, in the mid 19th century, it had aspirations to rival Liverpool in economic power. The town's brief period of prosperity was based on shipbuilding, and its Scottish founder, William Laird, engaged his compatriot James Gillespie Graham to create a plan that was intended to rival the New Town of Edinburgh. Its heart was Hamilton Square, one of the most magnificent residential squares in England. In the 1840s, when Joseph Paxton converted 92 hectares into the UK's first municipal park, and the great series of enclosed docks were opened, hopes were high. But the ambition failed, for the grandeur of the great grid iron town plan was impractical, and the long wide streets were soon built up with rows of brick cottages, no different from the workers' houses of Liverpool. 150 years later, grand plans for Birkenhead are once again in the air. With the recent acquisition by Peel Holdings of the Birkenhead Docks, a £4.5 billion regeneration project has been launched for the Wirral waterfront. Named Wirral Waters, it is to be centred on a cluster of skyscrapers that take advantage of some of the country's finest urban views.

Birkenhead and the adjoining town of Wallasey merge around the great series of enclosed docks, but both have their own separate identities. The centrepiece of Hamilton Square is Birkenhead Town Hall, a robust expression of municipal pride when it was erected in 1887. Yet it was spectacularly upstaged in 1920 by Wallasey Town Hall, which looks out towards Liverpool on an elevated plateau high above the river at Seacombe. With its tower derived from the Mausoleum of Hallicarnassos, built in 353BC as a tomb for King Mausolos by his widow, and one of the seven wonders of the Ancient World, Wallasey's building was chosen to act as the civic heart of the new Borough of Wirral.

Once past Wallasey Town Hall, the open sea comes into view, and off the northern tip of the peninsula, on a sand-covered shelf stands the Perch Rock Lighthouse, built in 1830 to guide ships into the port of Liverpool. Since the lighthouse was built, the Mersey channel has shifted closer to the opposite bank of the river, and in 1973 the structure fell out of use. Threatened with demolition, it was bought for £100 by a local architect, Norman Kingham, who went on to rescue the adjoining Fort Perch Rock, which had also become redundant. Though the fort was built to guard the seaward approach to Liverpool just after the Napoleonic Wars, it has never had to repel invading ships, and today it is connected to the land by a causeway and municipal car park. Nonetheless, the fort and lighthouse are the landmark buildings of New Brighton, whose early developers, like those of Birkenhead, had grand ideas. New Brighton was intended as a fashionable seaside resort, and large marine residences with sea views were erected in the 1830s. But no great hotels followed, and by the end of the 19th century, it had become a place of entertainment for day trippers from Liverpool. Its high point as a working class resort was the first decade of the 20th century, when a great tower that exceeded Blackpool's in height was erected. But alas the tower lasted less than 20 years, and since then the town has struggled to find an identity.

For millions of emigrants who sought a life in the New World, the last glimpse of the Liverpool waterfront as they left the river by ship provided an enduring image. Whilst the Mersey no longer teems with steamers and ferry boats, the survival of the city's historic urban landscape, its pioneering dock structures and its architectural legacy are a testament to the international importance of Liverpool and the great river on which it stands.

MERSEY PEOPLE

KATE FOX

PHOTOGRAPHY BY COLIN MCPHERSON

The Mersey and its people – for hundreds of years it has been impossible to say which influences the other most. Without the river there would have been no port, no merchants, no ferries, no shipbuilding. Many of the towns and cities that were the cradle of the industrial revolution wouldn't exist, and countless lives defined by their relationship to the water would have been lived differently.

But the river, too, has been shaped by its people. Dredged, bridged and canalised, its natural flow has been changed to better serve us. It has been polluted by industry, and revived by a clean-up campaign that is the envy of the world.

With the Mersey in the midst of a renaissance, many 21st century lives are still entwined with it, whether for employment, recreation or inspiration. From ferrymen to cabinet ministers, policemen to anglers, their stories tell the tale of the the Mersey, the river that changed the world.

THE CHAIRMAN

TONY BRAND

Liverpool Pilotage Services Ltd

"My father's family's been at sea since 1636. My maternal grandfather captained the Queen Elizabeth during the war, and I thought I'd go deep sea all my life. In 1988, after being made redundant as a sailor, I joined a small coastal company, and the first remark made to me was "I bet you've only joined us so you can become a pilot". I never considered it before, but the more I thought about it, the better it seemed. I was briefly a pilot on the Thames before a job came up in Liverpool.

The challenge is getting the ship into the lock without damaging it. Atlantic Container Line ships are 292m by 32m, and we're putting them in a hole that's 315m by 39m. Your heart's in your mouth as you approach, but if everything goes well you feel like a million dollars.

Shortly after I started, I was on a ship out of Birkenhead. It was a clear, windless evening, and looking across at the Three Graces all lit up, I remember thinking; 'What a magnificent place to go to work'. There's nothing on the Thames to match it."

THE RIVER PILOTS

JOHN CURRY

Liverpool Pilotage Services Ltd

"I came straight from school to serve a seven-year apprenticeship. My father and elder brother were pilots, and my mother's family had their own pilot vessel in the 19th century.

You began as the junior lad, serving meals and washing up, and you wondered what this had to do with piloting. You worked your way up to senior lad, learning your trade by living on the river.

The river becomes part of us as pilots. We know it so well in all conditions, different states of tide, different heights of tide, different weather conditions.

The comparison I've always made is to the medical profession. The Master of a vessel is like a GP, while the pilot is the specialist with local knowledge who takes over when the ship arrives at a port.

There are many difficult pilotages in the world, but Liverpool is one of the most difficult, and for me it is the pilotage."

THE ANGLER

LOUISE CLARKE

"I've been going fishing with my dad since I was about three or four. I'm the only girl in our club – I'm the only girl I know that likes fishing. All my mates think it's weird that I like fishing at my age, and they all think it's dirty because you're touching fish. Even my boyfriend doesn't like it.

I just like standing there, watching and waiting for the bite, and then when it comes, reeling it in, and the fight it puts up. When you bring it in and see what you've caught, you feel so proud of yourself. I get a cob on if I don't catch anything. I caught a thornback ray when I was younger, and I tell everyone about that."

"We didn't go out far that day, and I wasn't catching anything. Louise got a little bite and her rod bent over. Anyway, she started reeling it up, and got this fish to the surface. All you could see was a big pile of thorns down its back, and a pair of eyes on top of its head. Louise leaned over the side of the boat and shouted "Dad, I've caught a crocodile!" which me and my friend were in tucks laughing about, because she'd never seen a thornback ray before. And I was as jealous as sin because I never caught anything that day." (Les Clarke – Louise's dad)

THE CANOEIST

CHRIS CLEAVER

Regional Access Officer, Canoe England

"I love rivers, I'm unable to cross a river bridge without looking over. I found the Mersey when I moved to south Manchester, and went straight out to discover where it went.

I first canoed the Mersey fifteen years ago. It was actually my first-ever river trip. The water was running quite high, and there was lots of debris floating along. We were accompanied for part of the way by a cow's head, which must have been thrown over from an abattoir. I fell in, and was sick the next day!

The Mersey's got a bad reputation because of past pollution, and there are other problems for canoeists such as derelict buildings, steep artificial banks, lack of access points and some dangerous weirs. But it's in the middle of an urban area with a million people nearby, so in that sense it's accessible. It's suitable for beginners, and above all, it's local. The river's noticeably cleaner now, and the riverside environment's improved too.

Over the last six years, I've been working to get more of the river available for canoeing. The Mersey was part of a pilot project that secured voluntary agreements with landowners giving us the right to canoe on a 28km stretch of the river. River Mersey Canoe Trail. The first race on the trail was added to Canoe England's calendar in 2007 – a fast, nine-mile course from Burnage Rugby Club in Heaton Mersey to Trafford Metrovik Club in Sale.

This puts the river on the racing map. Hopefully it'll change people's perception of the river, and will encourage them to use the facility that's on their doorstep."

THE DECKHAND

BARNEY EASDOWN

Mersey Ferries

"I sailed in the merchant navy for eighteen years, but was made redundant in 1983. My neighbour spotted an advertisement for deckhands on the ferries, and I thought it would do me until I got another ship. That was twenty-three years ago.

I tie up and untie the boats and make sure the passengers are safe and happy. One of the beauties of my job is meeting tourists from all over the world and answering their questions. I feel so privileged to be working in front of a World Heritage Site. When the lights are on the Three Graces and you're sailing into it, it's a brilliant sight.

In the early nineties we used to have football races on the river with three ferries representing Tranmere, Everton and Liverpool. One year my mate and I were preparing the boats the day before, and being fanatical Evertonians, we filled every fresh water tank on the Liverpool boat so that it would be heavier than the others. Lining up at Seacombe, the captain of the Liverpool boat twigged that something was drastically wrong – instead of lying with its bow up, it was lying bow down. I came on duty to sail the Everton boat, and the bosses were chasing me all over saying "it had to be you!". Eventually they pumped the tanks out, and the Everton boat came in last, which I was sick about.

I've probably heard 'Ferry 'Cross the Mersey' five times a day for years, but if you put a million pounds on the table I couldn't sing it for you. I can't remember the words, I just switch off."

THE SEAMAN

ALAN FEAST

"I chose Liverpool to train because I supported Liverpool FC. I attended the cadet training school at Riversdale Road in Aigburth, then joined a company called Ocean Fleets. Within a few weeks of joining them, I flew out to meet my first ship at Port Harcourt, and found myself up a river in the middle of Nigeria. It was shortly after the Biafran War and a day or so later when we moved the ship several dead bodies were churned up. Quite an eye-opener for an eighteen-year-old!

My first trips were to West Africa, but when I went to the Far East, Penang Island in Malaysia, that was something totally different. It was like a paradise island. I enjoyed Mexico a lot as well. Later on as ships got bigger, time in port became very limited. I think I caught the end of the good years when you could see the world as a career.

Shipping went through quite a depression in the 1980s and 1990s, but it's picking up again now. Going away to sea is a completely different beast today. Modern ships are highly automated, particularly the loading and discharging of cargo. The industrial process has been reduced, and a lot of the heart's gone. Those going to sea today certainly don't have time for much recreation ashore. Vessels are in and out of port within 24 hours.

I miss some aspects of going to sea, but you do tend to forget the times your ship was rolling its guts out at economical speed across the Pacific for three weeks, or you were in and out of five ports, doing seventeen-hour days.

I remember when I sailed into Liverpool for the first time and saw the Pier Head it was from a very different perspective than I was used to. It was a major port that had a major influence on the world. It always had an aura of magic about it, and I was fascinated with the place."

THE PUBLICAN

DAVE HALL

Landlord, Jackson's Boat, Sale, Cheshire

"I remember the first time I drove down the lane to view the pub, I thought there was no way a venue with this location could be for sale. Then I walked in, and it was practically derelict, with buckets on all the seats catching rainwater.

There's been a building on the site since the 16th century and it's got strong ties with Jacobean history. The name Jackson's Boat comes from Farmer Jackson, who used to ferry people across the river for a penny a time. Then they built a wooden bridge, which was knocked down and replaced in 1881 with the metal bridge that you see today. There was still a toll to cross the bridge until 1947.

The pub used to fall within Manchester's boundaries, and under the old licensing laws it had a half-hour later license than those in Cheshire, so the last half-hour was always very busy. We still have Grandfather Rights to sell alcohol out of the bedroom window during floods. I've never had to use them, but I think it'd be a bit different now, throwing a bottle of Smirnoff Ice out of the window!

A lot of our customers who stumble across us think we're on a canal. When you tell them it's the Mersey they say "it can't be, that's in Liverpool". You have to try and explain that it does go from one place to another.

It's amazing to come down here in the morning with a cup of coffee and watch the wildlife. You wouldn't think you were five minutes from Manchester city centre. This is the real Mersey paradise."

THE POLITICIAN

MICHAEL HESELTINE

"I'd been involved with Liverpool for some eighteen months when the riots of 1981 took place, and I felt personally responsible because no-one saw them coming. We had to take a very serious interest in the problems and causes, so I asked Mrs Thatcher if I could take time off from the responsibilities of Cabinet to literally walk the streets and talk, listen and investigate.

I loved the people of Merseyside, especially the children. It was like being a pied piper. They would come out in their hundreds, and get me to sign my autograph, which they then sold for 50p to their mates in school.

The Mersey got to me, it was enormously significant to the history of our country, and I felt a debt to that river. For three weeks my hotel room overlooked the Mersey. I saw this huge majestic river flowing through this great British city, and I just felt ashamed. This was the river that had given life to that part of England. Without it there would be no Liverpool, and yet we had treated it with total and utter contempt and disinterest. It was an open sewer, and I felt deeply sad that we hadn't realised what an enormous, valuable resource it was. That's where the idea came from, that we must make good the degradation of centuries.

If you have a stinking sewer running through large urban areas, no-one will take the opportunity to develop alongside it, or create jobs or live close to it, but if you can clean it and give it back its life, it becomes a huge beneficial force for good.

Now, the Mersey is on the mend. It is a generator of wealth, of happiness, of opportunity. It has got a long way to go, but I will always take pride that perhaps I took the initial decision to reverse the downward trend."

THE LOADINGMASTER

PAUL JELLEY

Shell Oil Terminal, Tranmere

"Three ships pass through Tranmere in an average week, each taking eighteen hours to discharge its cargo. The Loadingmaster goes on board and checks the ship, then we discharge the oil into shore tanks. We pump the oil through underground pipes up to Stanlow, where it's processed into many products and chemicals, lube oils and fuel oils, diesel and petrol.

Ships normally come from the oil fields of the North Sea, but we get ships and crews from South America, India and Japan. The crews are very proud of their ships. They try to impress you with the cleanliness and operation of the vessel. Swedish ships especially are like floating palaces, but a lot of ships now are losing their national flags and moving over to cheaper crews. As loadingmaster, you do have your moments, when you have to discuss things during the discharge that the Captain or chief officer might not be happy about, but you wrangle through them.

I've been at Tranmere for about twenty years, and traffic on the river's a lot busier than it used to be. It's the life and soul of Stanlow Oil Refinery, really. Without the Mersey, ships couldn't come into Tranmere Terminal, and without us they'd be too big to get up to Stanlow itself.

It can be bitter in the winter down at the jetties. When you go to berth a ship you could be standing there in horizontal rain, snow, hailstones for two or three hours. But you're kitted out with good thermal equipment. You couldn't get a better spot than our jetties. I've been out there a few times at New Year's Eve or Bonfire Night, in the middle of the river with all the fireworks going off, it's amazing.

There's always something to see here, we used to have a fox on site that would steal the manager's boots, and we've had a kingfisher searching for a nesting place along the side of ship. It really is a nice spot to work in."

THE CONSERVATOR

MARY KENDRICK MBE

Acting Conservator of the Mersey, 1988-98

"The Mersey Conservancy really began way back in 1626, when Charles I granted a charter to Liverpool allowing them to levy tolls and look after the navigation of the river. Ultimately, that navigation extended all the way to Manchester, but it was still the Corporation of Liverpool that levied tolls on shipping. The upper river authorities became rather fed up with paying these dues, so in 1842 the Mersey Conservancy Act vested the interests of the conservancy in three commissioners, who were to appoint the Acting Conservator. I know of no other harbour authority in the country that has a similar post. I suppose it was a good old English compromise at the time.

The role is about maintaining the navigation, and the way the river behaves. If anybody wants to do anything on the Mersey, construct docks or training walls, do dredging or reclamation, or to dump stuff in the river, they must submit to the Acting Conservator, who then checks that the proposals won't have an adverse effect on the river. The Conservator also carries out an official annual inspection of the Mersey and the Manchester Ship Canal, and submits a report to the Minister for Transport. The inspection used to include a slap-up lunch, but for the rest of the year you're beavering away in gumboots in the mud!

Before me, the job had always gone to an Admiral on retirement, usually the Chief Hydrographer of the Navy. By my appointment in 1988, environmental concerns and sustainability were much more important than when the Conservancy started, so my background in hydrolic engineering and geomorphology were appropriate to the changing role.

For me, the Mersey's special because of its geological and geomorphological significance. It's one of the few estuaries I've studied that's shaped as it is, with its very narrow entrance and the fantastic upper estuary that's five times as wide. It's unique and fascinating. Ignoring any manmade changes, the river is never the same for more than a few days together, it's a very dynamic system, always shifting its banks and channels."

THE SWIMMER

DAVE SANDMAN

United Utilities

"I'm a field service engineer at the wastewater treatement works, doing electrical and mechanical repairs to the equipment. I've worked for the company for 34 years, and I've been at Sandon Dock for 17 of those years.

This started off as a primary treatment works where suspended solids were taken out of the water. Now there are biological filters, and the sludge is digested, treated and pumped to Shell Green, where it's incinerated. What's left is clean and goes out into the river. It's a vast improvement on what used to happen.

The interceptor sewer runs from Crosby to Speke, and all the waste comes down here, to the tune of 50 million litres a day. I see the kind of stuff this plant takes out of the effluent, and it's incredible. I wouldn't have swum in the Mersey 20 years ago, but I'm quite happy swimming in it now.

United Utilities were asking if people fancied the challenge of swimming across the river, and being an idiot, I thought I'd have a go. I went down to Albert Dock, and they basically put a cap on me and said 'jump in'. Boy, was it cold!

We train in the dock twice a week, but swimming across the Mersey is an annual event – it's got to be timed right. My first time, a canoeist sent me miles out of my way. I ended up by the Pier Head trying to swim back up river against the tide. Anyone who knows the river will know that's impossible. I made it across and got out at a set of steps, but because they weren't the official finish steps I didn't get a time, so I was most upset. I'd have killed the canoeist if I'd got my hands on him. But I'd swum across the Mersey – not many people can say that. My best time is 22 minutes – if you can make it in 20-25 minutes you're doing okay.

People have this perception of the Mersey being dirty and horrible, but it isn't. It's as clean as a river in an industrial town could be. It tends to look dirty because it's turbulent, but that's mainly silt. When you're swimming you just see silt, and the odd bit of timber. I've swallowed enough of it without any ill-effects up to now."

THE POLICE DIVER

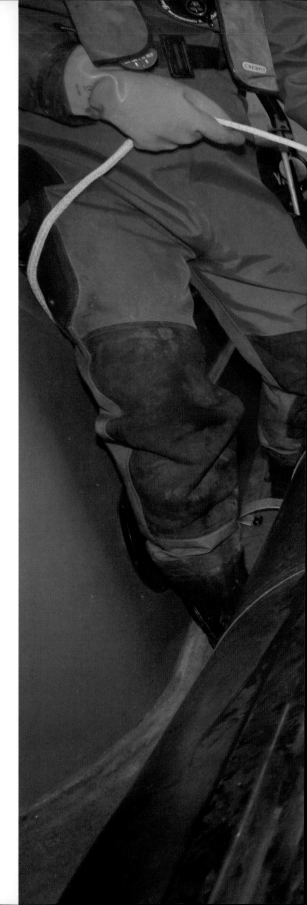

SIMON SNODIN

Diver, Merseyside Police

"I've been a police diver for seven years, part of a regional unit drawn from seven surrounding forces. Our main role is search and recovery – we're not a search and rescue unit. We look for bodies, submerged vehicles and missing people. We make some gruesome discoveries; I once found the body of a murder victim who'd been decapitated. Ironically, he was wearing a t-shirt by a well-known brand of sporting equipment that left a label over the stump saying 'head'.

The Mersey has a great tidal range, which makes diving very difficult. Slack water, between the tide coming in and going out, can be almost non-existent, and the currents make it hard to hold to the smooth hull of a ship, for example, when we search the outside of vessels on behalf of HM Customs and Excise.

A lot of work's been done to improve the water quality, but we don't see much difference in that respect. The Mersey's a very silty river, which is churned up by the tide. It's regularly dredged compared to the Dee, which is badly silted up, but there's a lot of sediment suspended in the water. It's very difficult to see down there.

The visit of the Royal Yacht Britannia in 1984 was my most memorable moment on the Mersey. I was in the Royal Naval Reserve at the time, as radio operator on HMS Striker. We were deployed as the guard ship, trying to keep pleasure craft away, when we received a message: "Striker, this is Britannia, can you go away, the noise of your engines is disturbing the royal party". So we had to limp away, letting the pleasure boats circle Britannia.

My mother lives near the Britannia pub at Otterspool Prom, so when I'm off duty I often cycle along the river from the Pier Head. My son recently learned to ride without stabilisers by practicing in front of the Albert Dock, and his little sister rides in a carrier on the back of my bike. Like many people on Merseyside, my roots go back to Ireland. Ultimately we wouldn't be here if my grandparents hadn't sailed up the Mersey to Liverpool and stayed."

THE REGULATOR

DIANE WALKER

Environment Agency

"For many, the river is out of sight, out of mind, so they don't think too carefully about what goes into their drains, and where those drains eventually lead. I just want to get out there and tell people that what they put down their toilet can end up in the river.

I work as a regulator across the whole of the Mersey river basin, concentrating on incidents and emergencies. On urban rivers you get a lot of culverts, so a pollution incident can be very hard to trace – you end up having to lift manhole covers on big industrial estates, looking for a needle in a haystack.

When I started, the rivers were full of sewage, but now they support a healthy fish population. Better screening has improved the aesthetic quality of the river too. Most people are not too interested in how many milligrams per litre of ammonia are in the water, but they don't like to see sewage litter strung from the trees.

As a regulator, you do take ownership of your patch. If an incident like a fish kill or damage to the aquatic environment happens, you take it very personally. It used to be a condition of working for the National Rivers Authority that you actually lived on your patch, so it's even affected where my children have been brought up.

As a family we enjoy walking along the river, from the source right down to Liverpool. When I took my eldest son on the Mersey ferry for the first time, he thought he was in France!"

THE BUSINESSWOMAN

SARA WILDE

"I was born and brought up in Liverpool, and always had a real passion for the place. It hasn't been an ongoing love affair, but it's definitely a rekindled one.

I come from a strong Liverpool family and my father was a politician here in the sixties, but I grew up through the 1980s and 1990s seeing quite a depressing side to the city. As I departed for university, I really didn't think Liverpool held many opportunities for me to come back to. It wasn't until I returned in 2000 that I saw its potential.

When cities are regenerating, I think you've got to focus on something distinctive. You have to understand what has made the city great, and fall back in love with those elements, then use them as pieces of the regeneration.

The Liverpool waterfront is not only iconic, but it connects us to a different time. On the river you get a real sense of the city's extraordinary past as a major port and a gateway to the world. You can imagine all the different people who passed through, the stories and the lives they led. There are echoes of that across the Mersey.

My first trip on the ferry with my dad at the age of ten was the first time I saw the waterfront from the river. I'd never even ventured across to the Wirral before. I was completely awestruck by the scale and grandeur of it. The first property I ever bought was a flat on the marina because it reminded me of being a small child and loving the river."

THE SAILORS

TOM WORKMAN

Liverpool Sailing Club

"Before the war, there was nowhere to access the river on the Liverpool side. After the war, a group of Liverpool sailors began searching for somewhere to sail from. They found a safe site at the airport and persuaded the Ministry of Defence to let them try it out. It meant lowering fifty boats down a 30ft cliff with ropes, walking across the mud and launching them. They did this twice a year at first, then more regularly. Someone took a caravan down and made tea, and they built Liverpool Sailing Club up on that spot over a period of forty years. It started from nothing and finished up with half a million pounds of clubhouse and a thousand-foot slipway down to low water.

We rebuilt the club because we wanted future generations to have access to the river. Most of us are now rather decrepit, and we're looking forward to a new generation taking over. We aim to get every Liverpool child on the water before they're twelve years old.

Kath's the hardest crew I've ever had. I never had to tell her what to do – she's always been able to read my mind. We like going up-river where it's quiet, untouched by human hand. The river's got an ever-changing face, with sandy beaches at the top end, and the docks at the bottom. Ten miles down and ten miles up, a vast expanse of water.

The beauty of it is when you're thirteen miles out at the Bar, and you can see the cathedral and the Three Graces. South of the Bar can be a very hostile environment, and it's a wonderful feeling when you see that and know you're home."

KATH WORKMAN

Liverpool Sailing Club

"For my first voyage, I foolishly offered to crew for Tom on an icy cold day, and he capsized me. It was disastrous, but having fallen in the first time, at least I knew what was in store.

When I became Commodore, it was frowned upon by other sailing clubs. "A lady? Are they going downhill?" But eventually they accepted it as the way forward, and many lady Commodores followed me. Getting women involved gave the club an added dimension, and encouraged more children to come sailing too.

Liverpool's waterfront is unique. It's been compared to Hong Kong, Sydney and New York, but being a Liverpudlian, to me it's better than all those."

THE ENGINEER

SHANTHI RASARATNAM, MBE

"My involvement with the Mersey began in 1996 when I managed a £200 million United Utilities improvement programme for five wastewater treatment works on the Mersey estuary.

I'd say that building enhanced treatment plants at Warrington and Widnes, on the upper reaches of the estuary, had the greatest impact on water quality in the river. It followed up the completion of the interceptor sewer from Crosby to Speke, which had got rid of about 28 untreated discharges.

What was so amazing was that we witnessed signs of new life returning to the estuary before our very eyes; wading birds like curlew, redshank and godwits, fish such as whiting, cod and plaice, sea trout, even octopuses. From time to time we saw seals, and on one occasion a whale decided to swim up the Mersey, and got stranded!

Walking down the Mersey now, I sometimes stop and talk to fishermen – without divulging who I am – and they all say that there are so many more species today, and even comment that United Utilities have done a wonderful job. It's very unusual for a company to get that sort of acknowledgement.

I've been privileged to play a small role in the whole success story, as part of a team of scientists and engineers. We also developed a way to turn the sludge from wastewater treatment into a safe agricultural nutrient – a technique that's been adopted by water companies from around the world.

One of the best moments was when the Mersey won the World River Prize for best clean up, beating the Thames, the Rhine and the Mississippi. But the ultimate highlight of my career was being awarded the MBE for services to the water industry. I went to Buckingham Palace and met the Queen, and I was able to explain to her all about the Mersey clean up, and how it's transformed the whole environment here."

CROSSINGS

DEBORAH MULHEARN

In the quiet churchyard at Hale village, close to the shore between Liverpool and Widnes, lies the body of John Maddock, drowned in the Mersey in 1819, aged 35 years. His is far from the only life lost to the river, as parish records show the names of victims dating back to the 16th century.

Hale is a sleepy village now. Yet in the 14th century it had a market and fair, because you could walk or wade across the river from Hale to Weston on the Runcorn shore. People brought animals and perishable goods such as Cheshire cheese across the Hale Ford. During the Civil War troops crossed with their horses and there were skirmishes to take control of what was a major crossing point. As late as the 19th century a local vicar used to take his horse-drawn buggy across.

The Mersey is a natural boundary but also a barrier. The name derives from the Old English words 'Mæres' meaning boundary or border and 'Ea' meaning river, and getting 'over the water' has been a challenge since earliest inhabited times. Before bridges were built, people sailed, were ferried or waded.

From the first basic stone crossings over quiet waters to the graceful bowstring arch of the Runcorn Bridge, forward thinkers have built towering viaducts that still stride across river valleys and innovative structures that lift and lower boats and vehicles, and take everything that needs to cross, including a cast iron underwater aqueduct that brings water to Liverpool from Lake Vyrnwy.

Around south Manchester, the motorway builders had to elevate bridges, not just over the river but also its surrounding floodplain. And at Stockport the need to bridge the high sandstone ridges above the river valley was met with a striking 111ft high Victorian railway viaduct. Later, in the early 20th century, the world's largest underwater tunnel was bored through the bedrock of the river.

People plied their trade on the river, carrying coal and salt on flat-bottomed wooden boats or barges between Lancashire and Cheshire. They understood the tides and the weather, but sometimes they lost their lives, just as people do on the motorway today. Familiar place-names such as Rock Ferry, Eastham Ferry, Fiddler's Ferry, Ford Lane, Stretford, and even Stockport, reflect these old connections.

In theory it was possible to use Hale Ford until the 1890s, when the building of the wall for the Manchester Ship Canal cut off Weston. When Graham Boanas, a charity fundraiser, walked across the river in the summer of 2006, he did it at a much wider point between Ince Banks near Ellesmere Port to Oglet near Liverpool Airport, where the river is two miles wide. Although he is 6'9", Boanas struggled against the strong currents, treacherous mud and shifting sandbanks.

The Mersey estuary, like a long-handled ladle, was too wide to bridge across its basin, which is nearly 3 miles across at its widest. There were no bridges until Runcorn, where the river dramatically narrows. The Runcorn Railway Bridge was the first to be built in modern times, opening in 1868. Until then, a ferry was the only way for the public to cross the river here.

Monks were some of the earliest ferrymen, as priories were often built near rivers, like those at Birkenhead and Norton. Ferries offered a more reliable crossing, though these were also fraught with dangers and discomfort. Daniel Defoe, the writer of Robinson Crusoe, made several visits to Liverpool between the 1680s and 1720s, and describes crossing on a ferry from the Wirral and an uncomfortable lift to the shore.

'Here is a ferry over the Mersee, which, at full sea, is more than two miles over. We land on the flat shore on the other side, and are contented to ride through the water for some length, not on horseback but on the shoulders of some honest Lancashire clown, who comes knee deep to the best side, to truss you up, and then runs away with you, as nimbly as you desire to ride, unless his trot were easier; for I was shaken by him that I

had the luck to be carried by more than I cared for, and much worse than a hard trotting horse would have shaken me.'

The Domesday Book mentions Seacombe ferry, and Liverpool's charter in 1207 included the right of landowners to charge a toll for crossing the river. These ferry rights were important privileges and were lost and won and fought over down the centuries. We are still fighting over tolls. Increasing the Mersey Tunnel toll (and proposals to charge motorists to cross the Runcorn Bridge) raise hackles today.

Old ferry slipways, stone steps, jetties, quays and piers remain. Some are still in use along the Manchester Ship Canal, which opened in 1894, and was cut to follow the curve of the river from Eastham as far as Flixton, where the two diverge. Dock workers cross and farmers move cattle and sheep on rafts to grazing land sandwiched between the canal and the river.

While thousands of cars and lorries a day thunder over the Thelwall Viaduct on the M6, which crosses both the Mersey and the Ship Canal, a little upstream, a rudimentary rowing boat takes foot passengers across to the nature reserve at Thelwall Eyes. A bye law states that 'intoxicated persons are not allowed on board', and that 'ferry passengers shall sit down and keep quiet.'

Where ferry points failed to develop after the Industrial Revolution, peaceful stretches of river were left. Fiddler's Ferry between Widnes and Warrington is one such spot, despite (or perhaps because of) the eight fat, belching cooling towers of the Fiddler's Ferry Power Station behind. There was a ferry here for 800 years (up until the ship canal was built) which took people the short hop to the marshy bank opposite, where prize fights and quite possibly other illegal bloodsports were held.

Arriving at Liverpool was a risky business, the first landing stage not
being built until 1847. The double decker Mersey Ferries as we would

Opposite The Queensway Tunnel linking Liverpool to Birkenhead was one of the great engineering feats of its time. Work started at both sides in 1925 and when both tunnels met in 1928, there was difference of less than one inch. Designed by Sir Basil Mott, it was opened by King George V and Queen Mary in 1934.

recognise them today date back over a century, to the early propeller-driven ferries. The Royal Iris and Royal Daffodil were introduced in 1906, though the 'Royal' prefix was granted after they served as troopships during World War One. Hundreds of boats were built for the ferry service over the years, with different coloured funnels for the different crossings. The Wallasey ferry boasted triple deckers.

Up to 1934 when the first Mersey Road Tunnel opened, the ferries were carrying nearly 35 million passengers a year. In 1947 the figures were still a healthy 24 million. The growth in car ownership coupled with Liverpool's post-war decline inevitably hit the ferries, and services gradually contracted.

The ferries still cross but are reduced – some would say – to a touristic travesty of their former selves. And the Royal Daffodil (in reality the old Woodchurch) has been pressed into bittersweet service cruising the industrial archaeology of the Manchester Ship Canal.

As Liverpool and its docks grew, travellers and businesses wanted more reliable and faster forms of crossing. Several schemes to build a bridge across the Mersey between Birkenhead and Liverpool were mooted. There were proposals as early as 1828, and in 1860, and then Warrington-born engineer John Webster designed an ambitious high level road bridge in 1892 and again in 1898. All these intriguing ideas came to nothing, not because they were outlandish ideas, but because of the high costs and also the politics and protectionism of the day.

More proposals came in 1912, 1922 and finally in 1923 a report recommended a road tunnel instead. As well as cost, the height of a bridge needed to allow shipping to pass under, the problems of bad weather, and its vulnerability to enemy attack in a country still reeling from the effects of the first world war, were all put forward as reasons to go with the tunnel plan.

Three tunnels are bored under the Mersey, one rail and two road, all within a few miles of each other and connecting Liverpool city centre with Birkenhead and Wallasey on the Wirral side. A rail tunnel had been suggested as long ago as 1825 to connect Liverpool with Birmingham. But it was not until 1886 that it happened. A trial tunnel was dug first, and then the tunnel proper was started. Workers had electric light to help but conditions were still arduous, with only pickaxes and explosives until a new boring machine was introduced. The opening was a great occasion but the tunnel was poorly ventilated and the choking engine smoke drove people back onto the ferries until the railway was electrified in 1903.

Queensway, the first Mersey Tunnel, was constructed between 1925 and 1934. It is over two miles long with two branches. When it opened people were invited to walk through for the price of 6d, and thousands took up the offer of this unique experience. At the time it was the largest underwater road tunnel in the world. Over a million tonnes of rock were excavated with explosives and pneumatic drills. Seventeen workers were killed. It appears semi-circular when you drive through it, but it is actually circular. The bottom half was meant to be a tramway – a scheme which never materialised.

The tunnel is not only an incredible engineering feat but also beautifully designed, by local architect Herbert Rowse. The tunnel entrance and retaining walls at Old Haymarket in Liverpool city centre are in white Portland stone and the stylised motifs of winged horses and waves symbolise speed and the river. The tunnel's six ventilation shafts, three on each side of the river, are marvels of design as well as engineering. The gleaming curves of the retaining walls and the art deco architecture at the mouth of the tunnel must have looked spectacular when 200,000 people came to see King George V and Queen Mary perform the opening ceremony. At the opening the King spoke stirring words:

'Who can reflect without awe that the will and power of man which in our own time have created the noble bridges of the Thames, the Forth, the Hudson and Sydney Harbour, can drive also tunnels such as this, wherein many streams of wheeled traffic may run in light and safety below the depth and turbulence of a tidal water bearing the ships of the world.' Phew!

By the 1960s, demand was such that a second tunnel, Kingsway, was built between Liverpool and Wallasey and opened in 1971. It was opened by the Queen, though without the sense of occasion of the first tunnel opening, and it lacks the style of the old tunnel.

There are still occasional rumblings about the proposed Mersey Barrage scheme, a plan from the 1980s which was designed to run from New Ferry to the Dingle with a road across the top. The plan was scuppered by the operators of Garston Docks and the Manchester Ship Canal who were concerned about its impact on shipping, although two locks were included in the design.

Runcorn's Britannia Railway Bridge was built by the London and North Western Railway to shorten the route between Liverpool and London, though only by 9 miles. It bridges the Runcorn Gap, where the Mersey narrows to 1000ft and is an iron latticework structure supported on massive castellated stone piers plunged into the river. Its Runcorn end is named after Ethelfleda, a daughter of King Alfred who reputedly built a castle on the site in the 10th century. Originally people could walk across it along a cantilevered footpath to one side of the track, which pretty much put paid to the admittedly unreliable ferry service a dizzying 75ft below. When the Manchester Ship Canal was started twenty years later, it was squeezed between the piers and the height of the bridge set the precedent for the high level bridges across the canal. The Mersey was navigable up to Warrington at this time and the masts of tall ships had to clear the underside of the bridge.

If late Victorian bridges look heavy and over-engineered, this is largely because of the Tay Bridge Disaster in 1879, when what was then

the world's longest bridge collapsed in high winds. The inquiry into the disaster specified steel rather than cast iron columns for new bridges and engineers set about reinforcing existing ones.

Today, computer aided design enables engineers to build lighter and longer bridges. Where calculating loads and distribution used to be a case of trial and error, now it is a much more exact science and sophisticated structural analysis packages mean engineers can design safer, more graceful – and also more economic – bridges.

The most high profile bridge scheme over the Mersey during the next few years will be the new Mersey Crossing, a 2km double decker of a bridge planned to ease the traffic loads on the present Runcorn Road Bridge, or Silver Jubilee Bridge as it was renamed in 1977. When this opened in 1961, it was designed to carry up to 9,000 vehicles a day. Nowadays that figure can reach 90,000.

Built by Mott Hay & Anderson (also the engineers for the Queensway Road tunnel) the Silver Jubilee Bridge is the longest steel arch in Britain, clearing the river by 75ft, crossing the Manchester Ship Canal, and replacing the old transporter bridge. The latter was designed by John Webster and opened in 1905. It was something of a tourist attraction in its day.

After Runcorn the Mersey is marshalled by two canals, the disused St Helen's Canal on the north side, and the Manchester Ship Canal on the south. After a few miles it breaks free to dance around Warrington.

Warrington has numerous road, rail and footbridges across both the Mersey and the Ship Canal, including daring high level steel structures, disused railway bridges from the old Cheshire Lines route, and quaint stone and iron bridges crossing both the river and the ship canal in the pleasant suburbs.

The town's 13th century bridge was destroyed in 1745 by the Liverpool Blues – not Evertonians but soldiers loyal to George II aiming to

Right The Ineos chemical plant at Weston Point dominates the view of the Manchester Ship Canal and River Mersey from Mersey View, Frodsham.
Photograph Alan Novelli

prevent the 'young pretender' Bonnie Prince Charlie from crossing. (He did manage to cross further along nearer to Manchester — wading with his troops through Northenden Ford, now Ford Lane leading up to Simon's Bridge.)

The Manchester Ship Canal had a huge impact on the river. The original topography and course of the Mersey has been lost in some places. Near Lymm, where the River Bollin feeds into the Mersey, it merges with the Ship Canal and they follow the same course for four miles until the Mersey reclaims its own course just before Irlam Locks and low-lying Flixton.

Where the two run together, a series of swing bridges and high level railway bridges (some disused) allow trains and traffic across and shipping through.

At Warburton, cars travel through the exposed steel ribcage of a bridge high above the water below, the only road crossing for some miles. This is a toll bridge and will set you back 12p. This quaint crossing could not contrast more with the thundering Thelwall Viaduct, which curves high over the Mersey and the Ship Canal less than a mile downstream. It is actually two separate viaducts, taking southbound and northbound traffic. When first opened in 1963 it took 3000 vehicles a day; now that figure is around 160,000. The two viaducts were built more than 30 years apart and from below the difference is striking. Thanks to computer aided design the concrete piers of the new structure are far more slender than the chunky original.

As the waterscape moves from urban and industrial and the canal marches on to Manchester, the Mersey takes a quieter southerly route onto more scenic stretches with water parks and golf courses. Sale Water Park was created during the expansion of the motorway network and also to deal with the Mersey's floodplains in this low-lying area. At the Water

Left The extraordinary Stockport
Viaduct, whose 27 arches dominate
the approaches to the town.
Photograph Alan Novelli

Park's edge the Mersey passes below an array of bridges built for just about every mode of transport across the centuries. Crossford Bridge carries the A56, or Watling Street, the old Roman road between Manchester and Chester. Next comes the M60 motorway, a footbridge and cycleway, Metrolink, and an old brick aqueduct. The latter is Barfoot Bridge, built in 1765 by James Brindley to carry the Bridgewater Canal, not to be confused with the more celebrated Barton Aqueduct which carries the same canal over the Manchester Ship Canal.

The M60, built in stages from the 1950s, crosses and re-crosses the Mersey as it ribbons around the nature reserves, parkland and golf courses of south Manchester until it reaches Stockport ten miles east. Everything in this town of hills and brows, including the river, seems to have been extruded through the extraordinary railway viaduct, whose 27 redbrick arches have dominated the town since 1842.

WESTWARD HO!

ANTHONY WILSON

f I care to think about it, and for this book I care deeply, it should be no surprise that every phase of my life has been touched, sprinkled religiously perhaps, by the waters of the River Mersey. No surprise since I think of myself as a Lancashire lad, spurning the linguistic aberrations of some early seventies Whitehall civil servant, and as a Lancashire lad, it is this river which rises in the black-brown moors to the east and kisses the Irish sea in the west that flows right through my homeland.

I was born and spent my first five years above my Mum and Dad's tobacconist's shop on Salford's Regent Road. I look back to a fifties heyday when Regent Road was one of the great shopping streets of the North. And why? It could hardly be unconnected with the fact that less than half a mile away, just down Trafford Road, were the magnificent gates of the docks of the Port of Manchester, the designated terminus for the equally magnificent Manchester ship canal.

Without the Mersey estuary, there would, of course, have been no logical entrance for the great ships that went on to cross the fields around Warrington. Eastham, on the south side of Mersey Bay, was indeed the entrance to Manchester, our Ostia. Salford and in particular Cross Lane Corner where I was brought up, were the intentional and alternate universe to the great port of Liverpool.

Those tall stately African seamen I sold snuff and cigarettes to; I was told they were 'Lascars'. Real Lascars were in fact men of smaller stature recruited from East India, although the word had come to be used to describe any foreign or African seaman serving on British ships under 'lascar' agreements.

Age five it was off to the country and a pleasant new detached house on an estate perched on the side of Strines Road in Marple. It was the simplest thing for us kids on the estate to climb over a low wooden fence and head off down the steep sided, fern layered hillside, crossing a stone and iron railway bridge over the Hayfield railway line and then down an even steeper slope, encouraged by the sound of fast running water below, down, down to the Goyt.

There, just across a mossy stone bridge over the Goyt, was a muddy forest full of wonders. Beneath the ferns and trees, the remnants of old stone buildings would lie, wet, lichen covered, mossy and inviting to a curious bunch of pre-teens; and then great tunnels and unfathomable constructions of the same millstone grit. By the age of ten I had discovered that these were the ruins left behind by Samuel Oldknow, a gentleman who had founded his mill on the banks of the Goyt and even an orphanage; kindness or exploitation? Who knows; though history treats him kindly; "He was the zealous promoter of every useful and benevolent measure calculated to aid the progress of general civilisation and local improvement".

I did my first piece of 'adult' work in my last year at primary school, doing a project on Oldknow and illustrating it with blurry black and white photos taken on my new Kodak Brownie 127.

Those ruins were our Chitchen Itza; just like the Mayan remains on the Yucatan, these cracked towers seemed to grow out of the jungle and at the same time seem to be at the very point of being sucked back into it. Maybe it's the natural origins of the locally quarried stone from which these temples – to industry – are built but they seemed then as much part of nature as part of man.

And of course these discoveries on the banks of the Goyt were my first real encounter with the Industrial Revolution. Dampness is all. But for Samuel Oldknow it was more than the dampness that helped the weaving; it was the power of that water coming down off the Pennines. He re-routed the Goyt to feed the 'Wellington Wheel' which drove his spindles through an underground shaft. The underground stone-lined tunnels, from mill ponds to drive wheels, were the stuff of adventure and dreams for young kids like us. And grist to the Victorian marketing boom which renamed the biggest of the mill ponds as the 'Roman Lakes' and later went from tourist attraction to fishing mecca.

My next step towards the sea, took me as surely to the port at the end of the line, as the Goyt, would rush on, merging with the Etherow just beyond Marple and then deep in the belly of Stockport, the Tame, going on to flow all

the way to the sea. But it was only a short walk from the ruins of Samuel Oldknow's empire, in a friends house on the banks of the Peak Forest Canal (of which, incidentally, our old boy Samuel was principal promoter and chairman of the committee which financed and directed its construction).

It was December 1963, and I can clearly remember the Hayes family front room and that twelve inch black and white object/trophy that seemed more important than that coming Christmas, more important than the death a few months back of the American President, more important than anything. And maybe it was. With its knowingly 'art' sleeve, with its four moody head shots, it was, arguably, the first album. Yes there had been long playing

records around for several years, there had been collections of singles and cover versions, but there hadn't been a thing called 'an album'; the world, my world had changed, and it was this black and white thing that had come down the East Lancs Road via the road called Abbey, that embodied everything that was new and exciting in our life.

Give Andrew Loog Oldham the credit for knowing the world had changed; he burst into the kitchen of the Chelsea flat where the Rolling Stones lived, waving this two tone icon in his hand; "Start writing songs lads." "But we've just got these great new Chuck Berry tracks, Andrew." "Screw that, start writing". He knew history when he saw it. And this album, with most of the songs, self

penned by Lennon and McCartney, was going to change everything.

'With The Beatles', their second long playing record, their – and the world's – first album was history. The previous spring, in the school playground, we'd heard rumours that one of the sixth formers had a mate in Liverpool who was going to bring this new band over who'd just had a minor hit with a single called 'Love Me Do'. Excitement rose as 'Please Please Me' smashed into Number One. A visit from the Beatles. Too good to be true. It was. It never happened. But we were all in on the ground floor, poring over our transistors on a Sunday afternoon, so proud when 'She Loves You' stayed at number one for a record number of weeks. As if it was us. But it was us. It was youth. It was our youth. It was the revolution. And it came out of the mouths and minds of these four young heroes from the other end of the A580. No longer was Liverpool the place to board the ferry to Douglas and the Isle of Man. It had become the centre of the world.

Above Their Name Liveth for Evermore. The Beatles at the Arnhem Memorial in 1960. Allan Williams and his wife, Beryl, are on the left with his business partner and Calypso singer, Captain Woodbine. Stuart Sutcliffe, Paul McCartney, George Harrison and Pete Best (with John Lennon, the photographer).

Opposite Excited fans dance in the street at the opening of Rock Around the Clock in Manchester in 1956. *Photographs Getty Images*

And the role of the port on the Mersey is mythically acknowledged as central to this great spark of creativity. Rock and roll was, is and always will be about influences flowing over and around each other and the constant and most vital influences are always Africa and Europe. By 1962, the epiphany kicked off in Memphis by Elvis Presley had waxed old and cold. Rock and Roll had become east Coast High School pop; saccharine and empty. In Britain all you had were the low cal Presley copies like Tommy Steele. But the undercurrent which inspired Elvis and his confreres, rhythm and blues, race music, was feeding the hearts and souls of a new British underground. And the steady drip of this raw, emotional, 'new' music was travelling with the Gulf Stream, across the Atlantic.

I asked my friend Mike McCartney about the role of the port, for although transatlantic freight-trade had ceased in Liverpool by the late fifties, the passenger liners still made regular crossings to New York. He described this culture of R&B aficionados, a British working class version of Normal Mailer's White Hipster, clutching their rare imported R&B recordings. He told me how Long John Baldry, a London blues singer, would make regular trips to see him and his brother and their mates and they'd all show off the latest sounds from the US, brought in for Baldry through the Docks in the East End, while his new Liverpool chums would share their trophies acquired through those great docks on the banks of the Mersey.

When he explained this phenomena to me a loud bell of memory went off in my head; "they were young sailors who knew exactly what the demand was back home for these rare pieces of plastic."

Liverpool at the dawn of the sixties, a fresh vibrant youth culture based on the music of black America; and the chance to be top dog when you walk down the home gangplank. As Michael described these junior sea dogs, full of themselves 'cause "they'd heard these things before everybody else" I immediately thought of my first year at University and the Easter Term of 1969. I knew people who knew people who were in the Oxford and Cambridge Drama Group, an occasional touring amalgam of the two universities' aspiring theatricals. That Christmas they had taken Twelfth Night or some other Bill Shakespeare classic to New York. And there they had seen the movie, 'Easy Rider'. My God, they were the kings of the King's Parade. The hottest folk in East Anglia. They had seen the film of films. They could say things like 'far out' and 'do your own thing in your own time' and they knew how it should sound. For three months they were princes amongst men.

Just like those sailors returning to the Mersey estuary, laden with priceless gifts, not of frankincense and myrrh but of shellac and vinyl. And Paul and John ate them up, digested them and regurgitated a music that would change the world.

If you think of those first singles, they were centred on pop, with the R&B influence lurking only in the inspirational background. In fact it wasn't until the fourth or fifth release, the 'Twist and Shout' EP that one got a real feel of the vibrant, shouty, blues background to this teen combo. But that must have been George Martin and EMI smoothing out the early records because many years later in the late 80s, a lovely old sound man at Granada, called Gordon told me a story of how Johnny Hamp, planning a mini-documentary on two groups, a brass band and a beat-bunch called the Beatles, had taken Gordon to the Cavern with a tape machine. The piece never happened and it was in a studio session six months later, festooned with Liverpool Echo headline cuttings, that the fab four made their debuts. But Gordon told me he still had the tape and would I like to hear it. Would I?

Next day we go to the music library and Gordon puts on the tape. Cacophonous, messy, unbelievably loud and violent, well, noise. Unbearably exciting. And it reminded me of only one thing. The sound of the Sex Pistols that first night in Manchester on June 4th 1976. Yes, it was that fucking amazing. I was shocked to the core. And delighted. As Mike said to me, "After Hamburg, they had really changed". Robert Johnston went to the crossroads; the Beatles had been to Germany. Maybe both had sold their

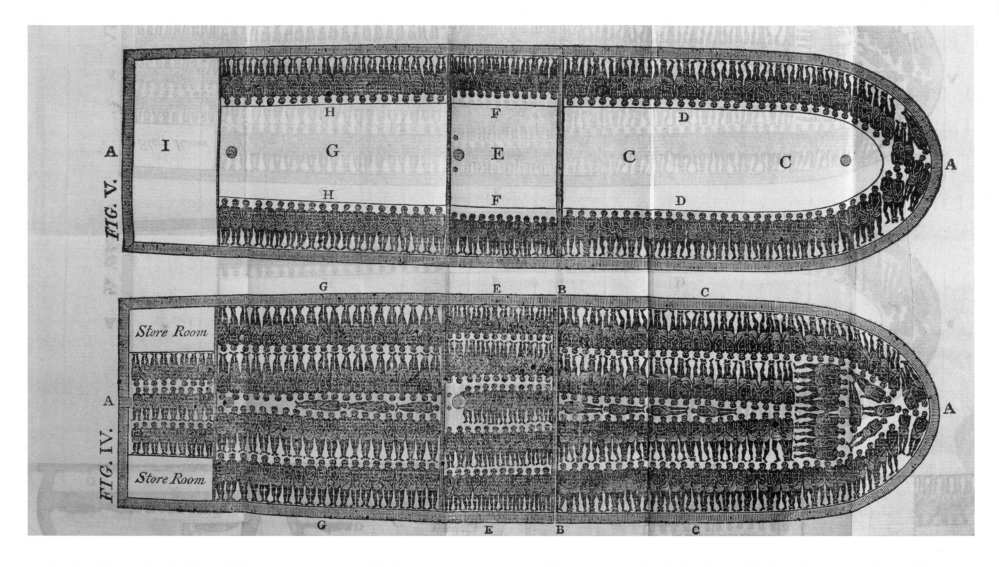

souls to be able to play the blues. Whatever, it was a good deal.

Old men and women, don't think that the Beatles and the Sex Pistols are the last time this happens; I saw a trance-emo group from St Albans, called Enter Shikari, on the 26th of October 2006 and they sounded exactly as exciting as Gordon's tape and Malcolm's band – which shows the true power of the culture of the plantations that found its way to Liverpool.

And therein lies the sweet and bitter irony of cultural history, that again, without this great river and its great port, none of this happens. For without the 18th century's noxious trade in brutalised humanity, there would never have been the blues and without those flattened seventh notes, no rock and roll. No life. No Beatles. To quote the Fugs "Nothing, nihil, nada."

And yes, the Beatles were never as bluesy as their contemporaries, the Stones or the Animals or Georgie Fame from Leigh; but it was still the heartbeat of the revolution which they led from the front.

Ah yes, Liverpool and the slave trade. Or rather Liverpool's. By the 1750s, after Liverpool had seen off the ports of Bristol and London and began to dominate the Atlantic triangular slave trade, there were two more Liverpools, one on the River St Paul in what is now Liberia and another to the north on Rio Pongas in modern Guinea. Both were slaving centres.

But it's somebody else's job to talk about these failures of humanity. Mine to recount the one truly remarkable by-product of those miserable journeys for so many of the people of West Africa. The creation of the music that has covered the globe for the last fifty years.

At first it was a bit of shock for we civilised westerners; "Why savages who have never developed a musical or other art should be supposed to have more refined aesthetic sensibilities than the peoples who have cultivated music for centuries passes my poor powers of understanding." H.E. Kriebel in 1914 used the word 'poor' rhetorically. In fact he was entirely accurate – his

understanding was worse than poor – and entirely misguided, as the civilised western folk who six years later were dancing to the West African Ashanti dance, or Charleston, could have told him.

The blues is only as old as slavery, or more particularly the end of slavery, for its profound development comes only with abolition and the movement of the American Negro into the world beyond the plantation. But it begins with the American work songs, which of course have their origins in West Africa. L. Jones, whose book 'Blues People' I will now shamelessly steal from (well isn't that what Eric Clapton and Pete Townsend did for heaven's sake from the great Blues guitarists) points to the music – songs – of the second generation of slaves and their work songs; "The African slave had sung African chants and litanies in those American fields. His sons and daughters and their children began to use America as a reference."

At the heart of this new American music was what was long misunderstood as primitive or the unskilled nature of the primitive (when will we ever learn?) seen as the strangeness and out of tune quality emanating from their 'crude' instruments. Classical musicologists spoke of the 'aberration' of the diatonic scale in African music. That geezer Kriebel quite beautifully describes the "tones which seem rebellious to the Negro's sense of intervallic propriety are the fourth and seventh of the diatonic major series." Ah, the flattened seventh,

Above A slave wedding c1820, an early American representation of the black music tradition.

Opposite The infamous triangular trade. Slave ships from Liverpool would take goods to West Africa and trade them for slaves, who were transported in diabolical conditions to the American colonies. There they were traded for tobacco, cotton, sugar and other raw materials, which were then brought back to England. The illustration is of the slave ship Brookes, in 1788. The lower deck indicates how 292 slaves could be packed. Photographs Getty Images

the augmented fourth. You naughty boys. It just didn't occur to these white supremacists, as we should justly call these blinkered art critics, that perhaps the Africans were not using a diatonic scale but an African scale, a scale that would seem ludicrous when analysed by standard western musicology. The flattened seventh, like the E-A-B7 chord sequence, are not the Blues; they are just faltering efforts of one music culture to define the other in its own terms.

For example, it leaves out rhythm, and though the Negro slave had to pretty soon leave out rhythm himself (drums were forbidden as seen as provoking passion and revolt – quite rightly) the syncopated patterns that had been used for communication, so much more complex than the primitive Morse code we westerners had once imagined as the use of drums, were actually the phonetic reproduction of words themselves.

Add to this the counter calling of the work song and its development into the repetition of the first three lines of the classic blues; add to this the rejection of 'beautiful singing' and the preference for raucous, husky, natural tones (and here all I can think of is the almost unbearable rasp of the early Dylan) and finally add in Emancipation.

As Jones points out; Slavery didn't create the Blues, Emancipation did. For it was only when this culture came out of the field, when there was no point in singing about bales of cotton or catching fish in a long forgotten Africa. The slave Diaspora spread to the cities and instead of writing songs for a work team to sing, it became songs for an individual to sing. It became personal. For all the incredible gifts of African tonality that changed popular culture in the West, the personal theme of the blues also lingers on monumentally.

Oh, Lawd, I'm tired, uuh

Oh, Lawd, I'm tired, uuh

Oh, Lawd, I'm tired, uuh

Oh, Lawd, I'm tired a dis mess

"So tired, tired of waiting, tired of waiting for you", wouldn't you say, Mr. Davies?

But enough of plagiarising the Mr Jones who did "know what was happening" and let me refer to my beloved guitarist Vini Reilly, the renowned

instrumentalist of the Manchester band, the Durutti Column, but also, to me, the source of profound mathematical insight into music (and music is maths and vice versa). He explained to me that "in our classical world, in a Perry Como song, the intervals are mathematically correct, they are logical and expected. But when you hear the blues notes, the augmented fourth, the flattened seventh, they are not logical, they are a shock. In simple terms they are wildness. You expect, deep down in your psyche, a note to go some place, but it goes somewhere else. You are surprised, you are shocked, and you are excited."

Vini went on to talk about Gershwin's desire to feed these different intervals into his work only to be frustrated by the solidity of a concert orchestra. Vini points out the role of the guitar where notes can be bent, and highlights the role of the bottleneck so beloved of BB King and all the white blues players; whether or not this was used because of fingers damaged by intense manual labour, certainly it makes the notes as fluid as the tonalities of their West African origins. He also told me about that other blues standard instrument, the harmonica, how the tines wear down quickly and notes begin to wander again allowing this all vital blending and distorting of melody. And then there's the chord structures that grow out if this non-diatonic system and inform the entire world of rock and roll.

And again Vini defines the unexpected nature of this non European mathematics; "a sound, a feeling that is shocking, that is extreme, that is at heart rebellious." How appropriate, how inevitable, that the sound of an oedipal culture is defined by the rebellious mathematical progressions of the Blues from Western Africa via the slave ships of the Mersey and the Plantations of the Southern States.

And how strange that my story begins in the hills below the moors, on the banks of the Goyt, with my first taste of an Industrial Revolution, and takes me downstream to the Irish Sea and to the two great progenitors of the Industry of Revolution that has shaped my life and, thank God, continues to do so.

103

DOWN TO THE SEA IN SHIPS

MICHAEL TAYLOR

Opposite A container ship passes Perch Rock lighthouse on its way to unload at Royal Seaforth Dock.

This chapter should be scratch and sniff. You can tell the story of the ships that come to Liverpool on the tide in pictures. You can tell the story in words. As I will have to do. But even today, the story I have to tell is one that hits all of your senses. You see, the docks at the mouth of the great river Mersey feed the stomachs of the people of the North of England. The thousands of colourful containers stacked up on the dockside may give no aroma at all, they represent the sanitised shrink wrapped, containerised packaging of supermarket produce that the public now needs.

But still, the smells of edible oils, cocoa, sugar and grain fill the air. And scrap metal too. It's what happens at the Northwest's largest working dock. It's how things are, much as it sometimes irks the fine folk of Crosby.

A grand tour – or a cook's tour – is a journey into the history of the port of Liverpool, but also a glimpse of the future of an asset of the Northwest that is widely misunderstood and widely unappreciated.

To scousers of a certain vintage, the heyday of the docks was at an indeterminate point at the high watermark of the British Empire, when as many as 100 ships a day would come to port. But ships were much smaller then and getting goods on and off them was labour intensive, slow, and wide open to pilfering. It would take 20 men two weeks to unload a ship. Today, container ships of twice that size are emptied of cargo – 1800 tonnes an hour – stuffed full again and set back to sea, and all within a tide's ebb and flow. That's why those that work there today tell you that the real heyday is now. The port handles more UK, non-EU, container traffic than any of the east coast ports, a total of 32m tonnes of cargo a year. The Mersey Docks and Harbour Company itself employs 800 people. But that's the tip of a large iceberg. Beyond that the whole maritime sector employs 15,000 people across 900 different businesses with a combined turnover of £3bn. It takes in shipping, repairs, warehousing, trucking, law and education.

And now that the port of Liverpool is owned by Peel, the company that bought the Manchester Ship Canal Company in 1972, it has brought into common ownership the port that opened a way to the world and the canal that was built to say – "stick yer tariffs". And a fine chap called Frank Robotham – he's the director of marketing – puts it like this – "what was once there to divide us, now unites us". He's quoting Martin Luther King, of course, but this is an emotional business. It can still bring a tear to the eye of a tough man.

So, to understand how the port of Liverpool works, the journey has to start at the place it all began – the Port of Liverpool building at Pier Head, one of the Three Graces. The building represents today what it used to be; the grandeur of an entrance to a major imperial city.

But enough of that. This is not a history book. And neither is this chapter. It is a love story, and a thank you note, to the fine people who have made the docks prosper.

All things considered, I'm glad that I took a trip in the opposite direction. Back into the city, down the river, but not as far down as the grain port of Garston. I was fortunate to do so on a clear day, with just a little wind – not too much – but more of that later. I also got to see the diversity of the modern dock and to take in the profound sense of constant reinvention that you see everywhere. If you took the journey in the opposite direction you'd see modern docks at the top and decay through the middle. It isn't like that. But then I had a wonderful guide. A lovely man called Eric Leatherbarrow, who used to report on local news on the radio. He still has a warm broadcaster's voice, even though he's now the head of corporate affairs for the docks.

The docks developed in three directions. North, to the sea. South, down the river. And across to Birkenhead, where the dock goes deep into the Wirral peninsula. Norse Merchant Ferries have two services a day to Belfast and Dublin with the services busier than ever. Heading north, Princes Dock is the first you come to. It's all hotels and office buildings now. And like Albert Dock, its use is not maritime any more. Visitors to Liverpool may think that's what used to happen here. But there's a glimpse of a maritime present and a shipping future. One of the shiny new office buildings houses the Bibby Line company, another tenant is Coutts, the Queen's banker – they know where the old money is.

Oh yes, the visitors. There are going to be more of these. A cruise ship landing stage that could enable even the majestic Queen Mary to tie up at Pier Head. The revenue from cruise ships themselves doesn't amount to much, but these golden oldies in search of a Beatles experience spend a lot. Up to $100 a day. And that's why the city is paying for it. Welcome all.

You don't see many more of the ships that sailed from the sea until you get to Stanley Dock, close to the tobacco warehouses where they used to lay out floors full of leaves. These vast, impressive, warehouses are derelict now. The low ceilings make it hard to develop into apartments. And then you see tugs, where a few are docked. These are shallower waters and the needs have changed.

This is also where the Leeds Liverpool canal meets the Mersey. Another waterway that reaches into Lancashire. And here the walls of the old dock look like battlements, as well they should; French prisoners of war from the Napoleonic wars built them. Behind them lay produce worth defending. Now they lead up to sewage works at Sandon Dock. Here United Utilities treat waste that is cleaning up the river.

A mile or so north and it's safer to take in the air again. The aroma is of a kitchen. This is the edible oils terminal. Huge vats of molasses, palm oil and vegetable oil are stored. This business is run by the American conglomerate Cargills. Their plant processes domestically grown rapeseed oil, one of the fastest growing crops that British agriculture has to offer. They also have a soya crushing plant.

Further up is the place where cane sugar once arrived at the Tate and Lyle sugar dock. The European common market put a stop to all that. Canada Dock is now used for animal feed, another scent to fill the air.

Stop if you've heard this before. This tale of what once was. Trust me, it gets better, but you have to understand how it all works. You have to understand that where once great fortunes were made, new fortunes are being made all over again. You have to get out and see these new mountains of great fortune with your own eyes. They rise like monuments to our culture. They stand as evidence of our desire to renew, recycle and make good from what we discarded. Ladies and gentlemen, this is scrap metal.

There is more scrap metal processed, shipped out and used to make new things from Liverpool than anywhere else in Britain. There are two companies making a lot of money doing it. S Norton and European Metals Recycling have invested over £25m in new facilities in recent years. Between them they export shredded metal all over the world.

S Norton's conveyor bridge at South Canada Dock can now move enough metal to load 60,000 tonne deepwater vessels – even the more regular 35,000 tonne ships can be filled to the brim with scrap in a startling 24 hours. Much of the scrap is shredded at a site at Trafford Park and transferred to Liverpool for shipping all over the world. Similarly, at Alexandra Dock, European Metals Recycling takes on tonnes of shredded metal, but mostly through a rail terminal, where 12 trains a week take the equivalent of 300 lorries off the roads.

The renewal of Mersey's dockside sites is a tale of tribute; a fascinating account of how old is replaced with new. The old docks that lie vacant could well be shiny new homes for ferry terminals to take more passengers and commercial traffic to Ireland. There has to be a business case for such a plan, but one barrier to expansion plans of this order is available land. And that's been sorted by Peel securing ownership of land all the way up to the dock road and up to Derby Road, the dual carriageway that links the Freeport at Royal Seaforth docks at the mouth of the Mersey, with the city centre.

The Freeport isn't much to look at from the ground. It's a secure site that needs certain standards of fencing, security and storage to keep safe the £6m worth of goods that pass through its gates every week. That standard requires virtually every nook and cranny to be covered by the most extensive CCTV system in the country. It's not only secured by technology, but the port has its own police force, funded by the Mersey Docks and Harbour Company. Businesses can store goods here without having to declare that they've entered the UK's customs regime. If they're subject to trade tariffs then it can be very handy to release goods from storage at Freeport, to get competitive advantage.

There are acres of storage and stacks of stories behind the harsh metal doors of the thousands of containers and warehouses. Take this one for example: Rubie's Masquerade Company, the New York based maker of party costumes have taken expanded warehouse space of 24,000 square feet to add

to what they first established in 1997. Behind a dark red warehouse door are batman costumes and Elvis wigs. They're made in the far east and stored here to then be sent on to those of an adventurous disposition all over Europe.

The others contain secrets. That's the nature of container shipping. No-one knows what's inside them.

This isn't just a quirky coincidence. This is as a result of investment, hard work and a slickness in turnaround that is as good an example of efficiency and progress as you'll ever see. The logistics park for the

Above There is more scrap metal processed and shipped out from Liverpool than from any other port in Britain.

Opposite Liverpool is the most efficient port in the UK. Lorries are turned around in an average time of 45 minutes. The Port has invested heavily in ship-to-shore gantry cranes to lift containers on and off with impressive efficiency.

Photographs Colin McPherson

container terminal hadn't had much spent on it during the 1980s. £23m of investment in new buildings, machinery and the necessary computer technology to log, scan and track goods means the lorry drivers can be in and out through the busy six lane gate within minutes, rather than hours.

Zipping in and out of the containers around the harbour is a busy fleet of 34 straddle carriers. So called because they straddle the lorries, lift a container on or off and carry the containers from dockside to lorry all day long. The rate at which lorries are filled can vary, but the measurement of success is the daily average of a 45 minute turnaround. "We're the most efficient port in the UK," says Eric Leatherbarrow, with a proud smile. "This is so important, because time is money and some of these truckers could be doing up to 4 runs a day around the Northwest," he says.

But this isn't just about boats and lorries, there are trains too. The port has five railheads, each dealing with more than three trains a day.

Once the ships come to shore they have to get the stuff off quickly. The longest quay is 1,100 metres long but, however many ships there are, they have to get the goods onto shore quickly, or the ship will miss the outgoing tide. The Mersey's tide rises ten metres and that makes all the difference to the captain of an ocean going container ship — twelve hours stuck in dock behind the lock gates is time wasted in the competitive world of modern shipping. To do all of this the port has invested in five new ship-to-shore gantry cranes. They lift containers on and off all day long with impressive efficiency. These Noells cranes cost £300,000 each and are now the main means of moving boxes around.

Where does all this stuff go? Where do all these ships come from? It might be easier to ask where it doesn't. Liverpool is the major UK port for trade with North America with a dozen or more regular weekly sailings. Three new shipping services were added in the first half of 2006; one to Montreal, two to New York, one of which goes on to Charleston. One of these takes Chinook helicopters back for servicing. But you may not be

able to know that. It could be classified.

Containers now come in from Brazil, the far east, China, the Gulf, South Africa and all over Europe. A new lorry service cutting out a trudge through Spain and France has been established by Portuguese hauliers.

From the top of the grain store you can see the range of services sprawling below. It was a still day — like I said earlier — so there was no risk of being blown off the top. From here you can see stacks of beans ordered by Heinz, to be baked in Wigan and canned for a nation of bean eaters. The Baco-Liner service to west Africa was restored in 2005, once again opening up the trade in cocoa to Cadbury's chocolate factories in England and Wales. A special £1.5m warehouse built by B&P Commodities provides a temporary home for all of this.

More and more produce now comes in a container. Take the forestry products that have always come down the Mersey. They used to come in ships full of logs and pallets of timber, much of it from Western Canada. Now the likelihood is that the wood will come in containers full of paper, board, plywood and panels. 2,000 cubic metres of plywood from China alone.

At the very top of the dock is the future. Plans are well advanced to build a new dock at Gladstone Dock, at the point where the river has a channel that is deep enough at 16 metres to take the new vast container vessels that sail the oceans. These beasts — they call them post-Panamax ships — can carry 15,000 containers. The proposed port, which will need £80m of investment, filling in an unused triangle at the north end of the present dock will be able to take two of these at a time and have a 17 hectare terminal to move and store the containers. It's to protect the present and invest in the future. Even at the current rate of growth of container traffic — expected to swell from 650,000 to 800,000 units in the future — there's a need to cater for more. This should secure an even brighter future and a wider, richer mix of smells.

WILD MERSEY

CHRIS BAINES

Opposite For much of the past 200 years, the lowland sections of the river have been as good as dead because of industrialisation. Twenty years ago, the Mersey was the most polluted river in Europe. Now, a sustained clean-up is bringing new life back at a rate no-one could have foreseen at that time.

The source of the Mersey is less than seventy miles from the sea, but it rises in surroundings that could hardly differ more from the docks and sprawling suburbs of lowland Merseyside. The heather moorland is a wild and windswept landscape, haunted by the cry of the curlew and the indignant "go-back, go-back, go-back" of the red grouse. Blankets of sphagnum moss soak up the rain, build up the peat and offer a toe hold for wild plants such as cotton grass, sundew and bilberry. A few rare moths and beetles share the habitat, and this is summer nesting territory for birds such as the golden plover, the oyster catcher and the redshank, as well as the curlew.

The streams of the Mersey's gathering grounds once flowed through entirely unpolluted, undeveloped countryside all the way from the hills to the Irish Sea. For much of the past 200 hundred years that ecological connection has been badly damaged. Building mills and dams on the river's upper reaches probably had relatively little impact on the wildlife. Indeed species like frogs and dragonflies would actually have benefited.

Draining the river valley's lowland bogs and reed beds would also have increased the range and quantity of Merseyside wildlife. As farmers' fields replaced the mossland, birds such as reed buntings, marsh harriers and bitterns would have become scarcer, but they would have made way for many more skylarks, lapwings, partridges and crows. In the early days, this cultivation of the farmland would also have triggered a great increase in colourful cornfield weeds, though most of them have long since disappeared.

It was pollution that wiped out most of the wildlife in and around the Mersey. From the early 19th century onwards the lowland stretches of the river were surrounded by some of the most unforgiving chemical industries in the world. As a consequence, for most of the last 200 years the river was as good as dead. Whilst birds continued to negotiate the valleys from the moorland to the sea, the fish life disappeared; even as recently as the late 1980s the 'soap suds' of Warrington's Howley Weir continued to advertise the poor state of the river.

There are still occasional chemical spills. In the past few years, organic lead from one industrial source was shown to have killed large numbers of small wading birds, whilst in the mid 1990s, the much-publicised oil spill from Shell's Stanlow petrochemical works wreaked ecological havoc all the way down stream. Nevertheless, the river is making a near miraculous recovery.

Peter Jones works for the Environment Agency and he has spent his whole life around the estuary. As a keen sailor, he remembers "racing the rafts of raw sewage" only twenty years ago. In those days, the Mersey was still thought to be the most polluted estuary in Europe. Today, Jones and his colleagues can quote records of about fifty fish species taken from the Mersey's waters. He admits that most of them are still only occasional visitors. The impressive swordfish that now resides in a Liverpool museum was probably a one-off, but there are at least ten species that have become firmly re-established in the river and its estuary. Not so long ago, there were none.

For Peter Jones, the salmon is perhaps the iconic success story. Two centuries ago, wild salmon netted in the Mersey were a staple diet in the region's workhouses – so common that the parish poor complained and called for something less monotonous. Now, after a very lengthy absence, the wild salmon has returned and, although it is still a relative rarity, there could be no better witness to the Mersey clean-up. These North Atlantic travellers are now spawning in the River Goyt, one of the Mersey basin's tributaries. In theory this should be impossible, since Jones admits that there are still serious physical barriers in some stretches of the river – but it seems the salmon have bypassed the obstacles by making use of the Manchester Ship Canal as a route between the open sea and the upper reaches of the river.

There are still serious problems for the Mersey's fish. Jones quotes growing concern about the chemicals known as endocrine disrupters. They reach the river from a range of sources such as discarded plastics and they are known to affect gender-change in some fish. The flounders of the Mersey seem to be particularly susceptible and, at present, the problem is relatively poorly understood. DDT was first manufactured on the banks of the Mersey in the 1940s. This and other long-lived toxic chemicals still pose a serious threat when any sediment in which they lie is stirred up by natural changes to the river's currents, or by building new structures beyond the water's edge.

All in all, Jones is optimistic. He has seen the Mersey and its fish stock improve out of all recognition throughout his career and, whilst it may be difficult to see the growing shoals of fish beneath the surface, there are kingfishers and cormorants, otters, grey seals and other predators to serve as more visible proof that this river is most definitely on the mend.

The industrial legacy of Merseyside caused problems for the river's aquatic wildlife. For the surrounding landscape, it yielded a surprising ecological bonus. Waste tipping and chemical pollution may have wiped out much of the natural habitat, but the hostile new ground conditions have proved ideal for some spectacular species. Lime-tolerant early purple and pyramidal orchids have colonised some of the chemical waste tips in spectacular numbers. Where mineral workings have collapsed, frogs and newts and wetland wildflowers have populated the resulting pools and marshy ground. Less toxic post-industrial land has proved ideal for trees and shrubs such as goat willow, ash and silver birch, and young pioneer woodland has cropped up on sites throughout industrial Merseyside.

The landscape's natural capacity for healing scars has been enthusiastically embraced here and, since the 1970s, Liverpool and its neighbours have produced world class ecological research and technical innovation. At Liverpool University, studies of vegetation growing in the toughest circumstances inspired a naturalistic approach to land reclamation that has re-established wildlife habitat on damaged landscapes all around the world. Building on this experience, the first of England's Groundwork Trusts

took root in St Helens and, by the early 1980s, extensive areas of derelict land were being successfully reclaimed in partnership with local people.

The charity Landlife started even earlier. Known in the mid 1970s as the Rural Preservation Association, this ground-breaking voluntary organisation embarked on a revolutionary campaign to re-establish wildflowers in the very heart of inner city Liverpool. They enjoyed early success by sowing poppies, cornflowers and corn-marigolds directly onto demolition rubble and, whilst this may have shocked the conservation establishment, it certainly captured the public's imagination. Landlife has helped to reintroduce a whole generation to the colour and beauty of nature on the doorstep. Their wildflower centre in Knowsley's Court Hey Park is a great success and growing numbers of their reclamation sites are now alive with butterflies and grasshoppers – and local kids.

Of all the people on the Earth today, one in a hundred lives in the British Isles and this is one of the country's most crowded corners. Nevertheless, anyone flying over Liverpool, Birkenhead, Widnes, Warrington or Greater Manchester can look down on an almost seamless canopy of trees and greenery – a living tapestry of parks and gardens, tree-lined avenues, school grounds and cemeteries. There are nearly a million private gardens in the Mersey basin, many of them with garden ponds and bird feeders and nesting boxes. With their rich mixture of flowering plants and fruiting shrubs they offer shelter and a natural food supply for many different birds and insects. These garden glades within the shelter of the urban forest are also becoming the habitat of choice for species such as hedgehogs, squirrels, toads and foxes.

One reason for the wildlife success of domestic gardens is the joined-up nature of the urban landscape. A complex network of green corridors helps to weave the landscape tapestry together. The streams and smaller rivers obviously play a valuable role, but two and a half centuries of industrialisation have added other corridors to the network. The first

Opposite top left Dunlin, knot and redshank share a riverside rock.
Photograph Guy Huntington

Top right A sparrowhawk at Stanlow oil refinery.

Bottom left Purple orchids have colonised waste land on the river
banks in encouraging numbers. Photograph Guy Huntington

Bottom right The return of salmon in numbers to the river is one of
the best indicators of improved water quality.

commercial canal in the country was constructed here, along the Sankey Valley, back in 1757 and the Manchester Ship Canal was built on the south bank of the Mersey in order to bypass the tidal estuary and enable ocean-going freight liners to travel far inland. These days the canals are less busy with boats, but over time they have become extremely rich in wildlife. The anglers who line the banks are testament to the fish-life living there, but so are the kingfishers and herons. Each navigation has a towpath running alongside it – miles and miles of level walking without any need to cross a single road. What better opportunity could there be for getting very close to some of Merseyside's most colourful wild plants and animals?

By comparison, the railways are relatively inaccessible. The passing trains cause little real disturbance and, as a consequence, wild railway land serves as a linear wildlife sanctuary. The fox that raids the bins by night, the hedgehog that feeds among the flowerbeds, and the colourful butterflies sipping nectar from back-garden buddleia bushes – these species, and many more, breed in the relative seclusion of wild railway land.

Grand public parks are another important feature. Many have lakes as well as sweeping lawns, flower beds and shrubberies, and they are especially valuable for wildlife because of their big trees. In some ways mature city parks have come to resemble aspects of broadleaved woodland habitat. They are now a stronghold for such species as the nuthatch, tawny owl and tree creeper. There are woodpeckers and sparrowhawks thriving here as well as such familiar woodland birds as thrushes, robins, tits, blackbirds and wrens. Some old parks have good populations of wild mushrooms in the autumn, as well as butterflies and beetles, and popular creatures such as squirrels, bats and hedgehogs. Where park keepers make space for dead wood, fallen leaves and wildflowers, public parks offer a real woodland experience for people living in the heart of town. This idea of creating 'artificial countryside' within the city was invented on Merseyside. Birkenhead Park is world-renowned as the inspiration for New

York's Central Park and there are hundreds of towns and cities all around the world that can trace the inspiration for their local 'breathing place' back to its roots beside the Mersey.

Although Merseyside's chemical industries produced some very toxic poisons, it was the waste from the growing number of people living around the Mersey basin that caused the greatest damage to the wildlife. Dumping untreated sewage and other organic waste into the river uses up the dissolved oxygen as it decomposes and, as the region's population grew, the lower reaches of the river and its tidal waters died. The wildlife living in the water was, quite literally, suffocated. However, thanks to investment in new sewerage treatment works, cleaner industrial technology and a general change in the approach to riverside development, the tidal estuary is once more the crowning glory of the Mersey from a wildlife point of view. It serves as a nursery for the fish of the North Atlantic and a terminus for enormous numbers of migratory wild birds.

The secret of the Mersey estuary's particular ecological importance lies in the huge rise and fall of the tides – the second largest variation in the world. This covers, uncovers and re-covers vast sand banks and tidal mudflats twice a day and the hidden wildlife that is buried there provides an immense renewable food supply for many other creatures.

A walk across the sand and mud at low tide reveals millions of clues to the wild wealth that is living down below. Mud-dwellers such as lugworms and cockles leave tell-tale signs at the surface – small holes and waste-heaps – but it is the wild birds that really give the game away. As many as 15,000 pairs of shelduck now use the estuary. These big, handsome black, white and chestnut-coloured birds patrol the wettest, softest mud, sweeping their bills from side to side, sifting the surface, and filtering out the microscopic snails that live there in unimaginable numbers.

Colin Wells, one of the region's many keen birdwatchers, has been monitoring birdlife on the Dee and Mersey as an officer of the Royal

Opposite Oystercatchers, more
commonly seen in twos and threes,
search for shellfish along the Mersey.
Photograph Guy Huntington

Society for the Protection of Birds since the 1980s. He regards the recovery
of shelduck numbers as hugely significant. The tiny snails they feed on are
extremely sensitive to chemical pollution. They have responded very
positively to the Mersey clean-up and already a staggering one in five of
the UK's shelduck migrate to the Mersey to spend the summer moulting
months here before dispersing to many other coastal wintering and
breeding grounds. On occasion, the numbers are thought to reach 19,000
birds and the number is still rising.

The numbers of wading birds are every bit as impressive. Half the UK
population of dunlin – 40,000 modest looking little brown birds – are
known to winter here, along with similar numbers of another small brown
wading bird, the knot. These birds feed in large flocks at the very edge of
the sea, and they are constantly on the move as they chase the water's
edge. One of the Mersey's best wildlife spectacles is the clouds of these
birds, flying in perfectly synchronised formation back and forth over the
shallows of a changing tide.

Oystercatchers are much more colourful birds, with black and white
plumage and carrot-orange beaks and legs. Their speciality food is
cockles, and their long straight beak is well-suited to plunging deep into
the mud and opening the shells. They feed over the beds of buried shellfish
but they are also commonly seen in twos and threes, probing for
earthworms on ornamental lawns, fairways and playing fields.

The curlew is the largest of the estuary's wading birds. Long-legged,
with a distinctive downward-curving beak, these brown mottled birds are
well equipped for extracting the juicy lugworms that live deep beneath the
surface. When spring comes, these birds of the winter shoreline fly back to
the hills to breed – an annual to-ing and fro-ing along the length of the
River Mersey that has been a feature of the region for thousands of years.

Several other kinds of wading birds feed over the tidal mudflats – bar-tailed
godwits, turnstones, redshank, and two or three different kinds of plovers. Each

species has a beak designed to seek out particular types of mud-dwelling wild
food and the birds spread themselves across all areas of the mud flats and all
stages of the tide. However, when the sea reaches high water mark, safe
standing room is at a premium. Then the various different bird species are
forced to crowd together, side by side, heads to the wind, and wait for the
falling tide to uncover their muddy feeding grounds once more.

There may be as many as 100,000 individual waders in the estuary on
a winter's day, and there are many more that touch down for a few days of
refuelling on their journeys between arctic breeding grounds in Greenland,
Scandinavia and northern Russia, and summer feeding grounds as far south
as the coast of sub-Saharan Africa. They share their tidal habitat with huge
numbers of wintering ducks and swans and geese and, all in all, the
wintering bird life of the Mersey estuary is as grand a wildlife spectacle as
any in the British Isles. Officially, this is one of the UK's top ten wetland
sites, designated as a site of special scientific interest under UK legislation,
a European special protection area, and as a site of international
importance under the Ramsar convention.

If Colin Wells has one disappointment it is the difficulty of actually
seeing the Mersey estuary's wild birds. Many of the best low-tide feeding
areas are a long way from shore, or obscured by tracts of privately owned
industrial land, but he suggests New Ferry as one place where top-class
bird-watching is accessible from among the houses of this waterside
neighbourhood. With the development of webcam and closed circuit TV
technology it is easier to show people just how much birdlife there is on the
estuary's far horizons; but nothing quite compares with the real experience
of watching wild birds with the wind in your face and your feet in the mud.

THE FLOW OF EVENTS

PAUL UNGER

Opposite By the 1980s, Liverpool was in crisis. The population was falling by 10,000 a year, factories were closing by the week and the failure to invest in the physical environment was plain to sea. The disused liner terminal at Princes Dock (left) was just one manifestation of the faded glory of what was once the 'second city of Empire'.

Making his home in the Atlantic Tower Hotel, and his temporary office in the Royal Liver Building, Michael Heseltine overlooked the River Mersey in the summer of 1981. "Alone, every night, when the meetings were over and the pressure was off," Heseltine remembered "I would stand with a glass of wine, looking out at the magnificent view over the river and ask myself what had gone wrong for this great English city ... In truth, everything had gone wrong."

Then Secretary of State for the Environment, Heseltine had headed north to Liverpool in the smouldering aftermath of the Toxteth riots. Two weeks of rioting, looting and arson by some of the poorest people in the city left one young man dead, hundreds of police and unknown numbers of civilians injured, and caused great damage to the neighbourhood's public buildings, homes and shops.

Heseltine was uneasy about the short-term social effects of the policies being pursued by the Treasury: "I was alarmed by the suddenness and extent of these manifestations of arson and violence. Besides, I felt that I bore much of the responsibility. I had been Secretary of State for two years. I had chosen to take a particular interest in Liverpool. I asked Mrs Thatcher to allow me to spend some two to three weeks away from day-to-day departmental duties while I concentrated on Merseyside ... I intended to find out what had gone wrong."

Liverpool certainly needed something. The post-war population of 800,000 had shrunk to 450,000 and was continuing to fall by 10,000 per year. Between 1966 and 1977, 350 factories closed or transferred production elsewhere with the loss of 40,000 jobs. At the same time, the port continued its decline. Its share of total UK imports and exports almost halved from 15 to 8% and its workforce fell from 25,000 in 1945 to 3,000 by the mid-1980s.

The Mersey was a filthy joke. For more than 100 years raw sewage had been dumped unchecked into its waters, from its source to its estuary. There were nearly 50 sewage outfalls in the lower estuary alone. Upstream heavy pollution entered the river from Warrington, Runcorn, Widnes and Ellesmere Port. The Manchester Ship Canal, little more than a stagnant strip of oil, caught fire in the dry summer months as the river beside it sweated and stank, hardly inviting for any would-be waterside property developer. The narrow, slow, shallow estuary between Liverpool and the Wirral peninsula took 30 days to clear itself of pollution from up river. It was not until the water authorities were set up in 1974 that a body even existed with the powers to make and execute a plan for improvement in water quality.

Neither Labour nor Conservative governments had faced the costly second part of the Control of Pollution Act 1974, calling for massive water improvement investment. After more than two weeks of meetings, and listening to as many local people as he could, Heseltine held a press conference in Liverpool. He announced 13 initiatives aimed at solving Merseyside's problems: a range of quick-fix steps to tackle immediate and severe problems. To see the list through to fruition, a Merseyside Task Force was set up, headed by one of his brightest civil servants, Eric Sorenson. Heseltine visited Liverpool fortnightly to check on progress.

A month after the riots, Heseltine presented to Thatcher and her cabinet a paper named from the most familiar phrase heard during those days in Liverpool; "It took a riot." His paper, leaked to The Times, suggested a single regional office in Liverpool comprising the main government departments concerned with economic development and a reassessment of urban policies for training, enterprise and redevelopment. It was ignored by Thatcher.

Peter Walton was a civil servant among Heseltine's task force, and remembers the issue of the river gaining in prominence. "Early in 1982 the question of the river kept coming up. He was asking: what about this water, this magnificent river?"

Heseltine brought forward the estuary part of the water authority's expenditure faster but was repeatedly told that he could not clean up simply the bottom end of a river system because there was still pollution coming in at the top. He had started at the wrong end.

On one of his regular Thursday visits, Heseltine asked how much it would cost to clean up the entire Mersey basin system and how long it would take. The answer came back that it was going to cost £2,000m and take 25 years. This was a vast amount of money for having a clean drain, and was not value for money. Heseltine wanted a more tangible benefit – development on land next to the river. The sum needed became £4,000m over 25 years.

In February 1982, Heseltine announced the go-ahead for the costly second part of the Control of Pollution Act 1974. A four-year programme in the Northwest would begin in July 1983, focusing on intercepting Liverpool's 28 raw sewage outfalls. The North West Water Authority's long-term objective was to raise all rivers to class 2, fair quality, capable of supporting fish.

By the summer of 1982, handling Heseltine's requests for information about cleaning up the Mersey and the benefits that would bring had become a full-time job for Walton, who remembers: "The Secretary of State kept bouncing back this request and that request, saying can you put a figure on this, where would it happen?"

"There came a point around the autumn of 1982, when it became such a diffuse, big request that it turned into a consultation paper and I effectively became its editor." Walton began to gather the relevant information on the state of the Mersey into what would be the seminal document needed for the recovery of the great river system. A now-famous covering letter from Heseltine invited responses from the public, private and voluntary communities.

"The haunting grandeur of the Mersey creates its own unforgettable impressions," he opened. "To earlier generations the Mersey and its tributaries were the essence, the life-spring of Liverpool and of a whole host of towns in the textile and industrial belt of the Northwest … But today the river is an affront to the standards a civilised society should demand of its environment … To rebuild the urban areas of the Northwest we need to clean and clear the ravages of the past, to recreate the opportunities and attributes that attracted earlier generations to come and live there and invest there."

Heseltine nailed the landward objectives in no uncertain terms: "From its source well to the east of Manchester to the sea beyond Liverpool we must aim for much cleaner water. It encourages the restoration to full use and beauty of the many waterside places neglected over the years … A Mersey basin restored to a quality of environmental standards fit for the end of this century will be of incalculable significance in the creation of new employment … I can think of no more exciting challenge for the decades ahead." And then he was gone, promoted to Defence Secretary in January 1982.

Heseltine's successor, Tom King, chaired a conference on the paper on March 18 1983 at Daresbury. The response was positive and strong.

"After that there was no going back," Walton says. "The instinct normally in the civil service is to try and lose it to the local authorities if it's getting too big for us, but I just hung on by my nails and thought 'this is wonderful'."

By the time the final approval from London was called for, there had been another change in command and Patrick Jenkin was Secretary of State for the Environment. Jenkin agreed there should be an organisation, although the question of resources was left a bit vague.

By May 1983, politics in Liverpool was dominating national debate. The Liverpool Labour Party took control of Liverpool City Council, and the infamous ideological battle between Labour's Militant Tendency and the Conservative government began in earnest. The following year, the city's ruling Labour party, under the de facto leadership of Derek Hatton and Tony Byrne, refused to set a budget for rates unless further funding was handed down by London.

In July 1984, a settlement was reached between the Conservative

Right Bill Bryson famously wrote that when he arrived in Liverpool it was having a festival of litter. The uncared for attitude had permeated every aspect of civic life, with swagmen selling their wares out of cardboard boxes on what was once one of Britain's premier shopping streets.

government and Liverpool's rebellious rulers following concessions on both sides, although the defeated minister Jenkin, who had been slow and clumsy in reaching a deal, would not repeat his mistakes when challenged again in 1985. Liverpool capitulated and Hatton's militant 'republic' crumbled by 1987 when the leadership was replaced.

Meanwhile, funding revolutions were occurring on an even higher stage, one that would benefit work on the Mersey. So-called European structural funds were becoming widely used for schemes on the landward side. But as the volume of European-funded projects grew, organising them on an individual case-by-case basis began to overwhelm the European Commission. It wanted to move towards a programme structure, where Brussels could manage from a higher level of involvement.

When EC commissioners came to the UK looking for pilot programmes on which to test its new thinking, it found a ready-made prototype in the Mersey basin initiative. The Mersey programme received £60m for three years, which would then be repeated on a rolling basis all being well. Two-thirds was to be spent on water and the remaining one-third on land.

By the mid 1980s, the country was beginning to get used to Thatcher's penchant for privatisation and water was being touted as the next likely candidate. Yet the more money the North West Water Authority's projects received via Heseltine's new initiative for the Mersey basin, the more opponents to privatisation smelled a rat. There were lengthy and heated rows inside the Commission that this was a fix to soften up North West Water with a huge influx of money, to prepare it for privatisation.

The money certainly came in handy at the North West Water Authority, which began work in 1984 on a huge capital investment in cleaning up the river. At last the 28 raw domestic sewage pipes discharging from the Liverpool banks of the Mersey would be intercepted by a major new pipe and diverted to a purpose-built wastewater treatment works at Sandon Dock in north Liverpool.

The project would take five years and cost £300m to build, with funds coming from specially raised water rates as well as EC grants and a favourable European Investment Bank loan. Sandon Dock was operational by 1989, capable of dealing with up to 950m litres of wastewater per day. Discharge levels in the Mersey were starting to fall, by 30% when Sandon Dock started and nearer 50% by the time it finished.

Indeed, 1984 was a year for grand projects. Two of Heseltine's best-known 'babies' were born that year. Under the supervision of his Merseyside Development Corporation, set up by Heseltine in 1981, the Albert Dock, a wonderful complex designed in the 1840s by a great architect of the Industrial Revolution, Jesse Hartley, was restored and put back into use as bars, restaurants, museums, shops, and the Tate Liverpool art gallery.

The other great scheme of the year had even wider, if shorter-lived, prominence. The idea for garden festivals was simple, as Heseltine remembers: "Use public money to eliminate dereliction, and green the area to produce a high-quality environment. Stage a festival of attractions for six

months and then sell the much improved site for redevelopment."

Liverpool was not an automatic choice. There was a national competition held and the best bids were from Liverpool and Stoke. Liverpool would get the first international garden festival and Stoke the second two years later.

A former rubbish dump at Otterspool beyond Liverpool's south docks was the target for the grand makeover. With the full weight of central government money and machine behind the festival the transformation was amazing.

The first part of the plan was superbly executed and for nine months from the summer of 1984 crowds travelled from all over to explore the themed international gardens, lakes, pagodas and space-age silver tubular exhibition hall.

Above and right Amongst the initiatives proposed by Michael Heseltine's Mersey Task Force, none were more successful than the 1984 International Garden Festival. Contaminated, derelict land overlooking the river was transformed into a magnificent landscape of gardens, lakes, pagodas and pavilions, attracting millions of visitors from all over the world.

By 1985 the foundations were set for the official launch of the Mersey Basin Campaign. An inaugural chairman had been found in John Tavare, a successful businessman about to retire from his small manufacturing conglomerate based in Cheshire, and a former chairman of the Northwest branch of the CBI. Excited, inspirational, as mercurial as Heseltine in many ways, Tavare (capably succeeded later by Brian Alexander, Joe Dwek and Peter Batey) followed his pattern of leadership through charisma, charm and cajoling.

While the consultation paper in 1982 was the intellectual birth, 1985 was the formal birth of the campaign. The clock started counting down 25 years from here. The £4bn cost (£2.5bn on water, £1.5bn on land) would mount up from here. The campaign had a focal point, the river. All the partners had to do was stop polluting. If they stopped abusing the river it would naturally recover, as rain fell and flowed out.

Local people could see the clean banks and enjoy the new country parks but not the hidden treatment works. If the local sewerage works were no longer dumping straight into the river then a virtuous cycle would start. The property developers would cease to be put off by debris, stench and oil and communities may turn and face the water again. Otherwise it would be back to Heseltine's question at the outset: what's the benefit of clean water? There is no point having a clean river if development does not come with it.

That landward progress could run ahead of water improvement was shown in Salford Quays in 1985, with the publication of a plan to redevelop hundreds of acres of derelict dockland on the Manchester Ship Canal. Salford was among several Greater Manchester authorities which had used the government's Derelict Land Grant to great effect and decided to have one almighty push at Salford Quays. Offices, retail, cinemas, hotels, housing, all would help build a new urban community over the course of a generation.

For once the property interest acted as a pressure to plead for better quality water in Salford Quays. The polluted water from the Ship Canal was separated off by bunds across the docks and a mixing system was installed to improve the water quality. Fish stocking took place. Two new canals and a lock entrance were constructed for boats to navigate. New roads and pedestrian bridges were constructed, along with promenades and low jetties for smaller boats.

After a long and controversial fight, the publicly listed Manchester Ship Canal Company was bought in 1987 by John Whittaker and his family. Whittaker's Peel Holdings, a property firm set up a decade earlier, became a major player in both the landward and water sides of the story of the reborn Mersey.

Whittaker's deal in 1987 saw him take control of a port, a canal and 3,000 acres of land including large parts of Salford Quays and the area where he would build the shopping behemoth of the Trafford Centre ten years later. Peel would became crucial to joining up the assets of the Mersey and realising their potential.

Privatisation of the water industry was finally pushed through in 1989. The North West Water Authority was split into the newly created United Utilities while the regulatory side became part of the new National Rivers Authority.

United Utilities was charged with spending vast amounts upgrading its infrastructure across its entire patch, much wider than the Mersey basin area. By 2005 it had spent £8bn replacing and repairing treatments works and the network of pipes and sewers. Today, the waters of the Mersey and the Northwest are cleaner than at any time since the start of the Industrial Revolution more than 100 years ago.

No sooner had water privatisation been achieved than Thatcher, its architect and Prime Minister since 1979, was ousted by her own party in 1990. Heseltine was back. Now under the premiership of John Major, he once more became Secretary of State for the Environment.

When the first major review of the campaign's performance was published in 1995 the results were overwhelming. Water quality at Howley Weir in Warrington, the freshwater limit of the Mersey, showed dissolved oxygen saturation had risen from 10% in 1962 to more than 70% in 1993. Water quality there was still Class 3 (poor) but much nearer the desired Class 2 (fair) or above. The National Rivers Authority found slow but steady improvement in water quality across the Mersey basin. Class 1 and 2 rivers and canals had increased at the expense of Class 3 and 4. In ten years since 1985, North West Water, now part of United Utilities, had completed 700 projects to improve water quality in the Mersey system at a cost of £720m.

By the mid 1990s European aid was changing and an altogether programme-based regime was coming in, having been partly tested on the campaign years earlier. The first round of the Objective One programme arrived in Merseyside in 1994, worth £600m in European grants.

Europe was also taking a firmer line with its water quality directives and, in 1996, the UK created the Environment Agency to tighten controls on pollution.

A period of change was cemented by a new government in 1997, with John Prescott becoming signatory for the Mersey Basin Campaign as Secretary of State for the Environment Transport and the Regions. A former merchant seaman with Cunard who sailed out of Liverpool in the 1960s, Prescott would not have wanted to change course on the Mersey.

Peel Holdings made another key acquisition in 1997, buying a 76% interest in Liverpool Airport, nestled on the banks of the Mersey in Speke, south Liverpool. Peel took total control in 2000 and renamed it Liverpool John Lennon Airport. European grants were used to build a new terminal and passengers numbers have soared past 3m per year on the back of investment and the budget airline boom. In late 2005, Peel also secured the takeover of the Mersey Docks and Harbour Company, operator of the Port of Liverpool and owner of more than 1,000 acres of largely undeveloped land. Of the missed landward opportunities of the past 20 years, many can be laid at the feet of the dock company, which sat on too much land for too long.

Water quality improvement was also helped in the 1990s by the rapid retraction of the chemical industry on the banks of the river with disposals by foreign owners and manufacturing movement overseas. Those plants that remained employed better technology, saving money and more often than not making environmental improvements as a result.

Strangely, Heseltine does not mention the river campaign in his autobiography but cites it repeatedly in interviews as his proudest achievement in Merseyside, if not politics. The recovery of the river is hailed as a great success. But how much of this would have happened anyway due to water privatisation or European pressures?

John Glester, part of Heseltine's task force in the 1980s and now chairman of the New Heartlands housing market renewal pathfinder in Merseyside, says: "I don't think we would be where we are today with everyone working together on the river without the start that Heseltine gave the campaign in the early days. He engaged partners who would have been at the back of the queue of volunteering if improvement had come about from legislation alone."

Certainly, there would have been no inspirational element at all without Heseltine, and progress would have been much slower as a result. The campaign would not have been a recognisable entity and the relationships between assets could not have been seen as clearly.

The campaign's success has been its pragmatism, Walton believes. "The campaign was never a blueprint, either in organisational terms or spend or programme. It consisted of the best efforts of the people available at the time."

Maybe, just once, politics worked.

RIVER FUTURES

STEVE CONNOR

Imagine it is the year 2050. The electrical pipelines from the Burbo Bank offshore wind farm have stopped pumping their turbine-derived juice into an increasingly marginalised National Grid. The 500 megawatts of energy that their re-powered blades and integrated wave generators produce is now flowing directly into the newly-converted Shell Stanlow Hydrogen Facility. Stanlow has been dedicated to hydrogen production for almost 20 years now, driven by the unprecedented demand for hydrogen fuel cells in transport, households and even small domestic appliances.

Things have changed dramatically from the days when Stanlow handled twelve million tonnes of crude oil per year and powered the rush hour tailbacks across most of the UK. All cars are quiet and come with cappuccino machines hooked up to their tailpipes as hot water replaces carbon monoxide in the resulting exhaust.

Sounds unfeasible? This scale of shift in energy production is perfectly plausible within a single generation. In fact, it is imperative. For the Mersey, there will be an increased focus on offshore schemes like Burbo Bank, as the analysis outlined by Sir Nicholas Stern's review of the economics of climate change makes the economics of wind energy more attractive than ever. At the River's headwaters in the Pennines, ill-informed protests at onshore turbines in the gustiest areas of Europe's windiest country will cease to find favour with the chairs of planning committees: if you want real visual intrusion, try a landscape ravaged by a five degree shift in temperature and a thirty per cent increase in rainfall.

In the coastal areas at the mouth of the Mersey and at the headwaters, change will come as renewable energy comes further into the mainstream but it is in the estuary of the river that the most dramatic new scheme may take shape.

If feasibility studies launched in 2006 are successful, new tidal power technologies within the Mersey could be delivering up to 20 per cent of Liverpool's electricity within a generation. With a ten metre tidal range and remarkably strong currents, the Mersey has more potential to generate energy than most rivers across Britain, perhaps even Europe. Co-sponsored by Peel Holdings, the owners of Manchester Ship Canal, Mersey Docks and large sections of Wirral's waterfront, and with the support of the Northwest Regional Development Agency, a study is underway to consider options which could include a tidal fence with turbines or even a giant modern version of a water wheel measuring 30 metres in diameter. A number of technologies are still being considered, but the scheme, if it comes to fruition, would become one of the largest energy generators in the country.

Peel Holding's plans for tidal power are advanced and ambitious but they are certainly not the only show in town. Back up the Mersey and the 'Manchester Bobber' is taking shape at The University of Manchester. The innovative and patented new wave energy device has already been tested at 1/100th scale and the team behind it are set to build a prototype at 1/10th of the final envisaged scale. The invention will use the rise and fall of waves themselves to drive an onboard generator and produce electricity.

Energy generation will be a defining factor for the future of the Mersey but climate change will not wait for patents to be filed and feasibility studies to be published. The greenhouse gas emissions from the last 50 years are already in play and since 1800, the concentration levels of carbon dioxide in the atmosphere have risen by 30%. In practical terms, this means that we are probably already experiencing some climatic changes as the result of burning fossil fuels and, over the next half century or so, the impacts will get worse before they get better.

Along the River Mersey, this will mean a hike in temperatures during summer of between two and six degrees. Summer rainfall may fall by up to 50 per cent, while in winter the rainfall levels could rise by up to 30 per cent. There will also be a rise in sea levels by 2080 of up to 67cm. The overarching pattern will be one of extreme weather events and increased

131

intensity: when it gets hot, it will get really hot; when it rains, it will rain hard. Back in those Pennine hills that feed the Mersey, the rains will increase soil erosion and potential run-off into waterways; as the Mersey snakes through towns and cities on its way to the Irish Sea the risk of flooding will grow significantly; and at the mouth of the River a rise in sea levels and an increased 'storm surge' will put coastal areas at risk.

The opportunities that come from confronting climate change will bring with them challenges for those who manage, use or live alongside the river. They will have to adapt to the changes that lie ahead and build climate change into the very centre of their future plans.

Yet people living in the two great cities along the River Mersey – Liverpool and Manchester – have always relished a challenge, climatic or otherwise. First passenger railway? No problem. First computer? OK. How about bringing the ocean to Manchester and making a land-locked city the third busiest port in Victorian England? Time to roll up those sleeves …

Frustrated at having to rely on the Port of Liverpool for access to trade (four fifths of Manchester's trade passed through the Port), industrialist Daniel Adamson and a group of politicians, businessmen and engineers set about bringing the sea to Manchester in 1882. With typical Victorian chutzpah they raised an initial £5 million to cover construction costs, got an act through Parliament in the face of stiff resistance from Liverpool and the railway companies, and began building the eighth largest canal in the world on 11 November 1887. At its height, the project employed around 17,000 workers.

You know what they say about time and tide. Ironically, today the docks at Liverpool and the Ship Canal are both owned by the same company – Peel Holdings – and the latest challenge for Peel relates not to a factional fight between Liverpool and Manchester, but to a certain canal in Central America: the Panama.

Opened in 1914, the Panama Canal has become one of the most important waterways in the world. More recently, globalised trade has upped its game and a growing number of container ships – known as 'post-panamax' – are simply too big to squeeze through the link between the Atlantic and Pacific oceans. By 2011 it is estimated that 37 per cent of the world's container ships will be post-panamax. This is creating a headache for the Panamian government as it works to raise US$5 billion to upgrade the canal, but for Liverpool, it's a new market opportunity.

In 2005 the Mersey Docks and Harbour Company submitted its plans to build a new post-panamax container terminal at Seaforth Dock in the Port of Liverpool. The new £90 million terminal, given the go-ahead by Government in March 2007, will be the first of its kind on the UK's West Coast and will, at a stroke, double the Port's container capacity; it will secure Liverpool's current reputation as the most important port for trade with North America and give it the ability to secure other important lines of global trade.

The sci-fi sounding post-panamax facility is not the only new dockside development that will shape Liverpool's maritime future. In 2005 approval was given for £17 million in funding from the Northwest Regional Development Agency and Europe for a new cruise liner facility. Tall ships, naval vessels and the most glamorous of cruise liners will be able to drop

Above The increase in size of containerships has necessitated new facilities – called post-panamax – to cope with the new ships. Liverpool will have the first such facility in the UK, effectively doubling the Port's capacity.

Opposite With typical Victorian enterprise, land-locked Manchester challenged Liverpool's monopoly by building the third busiest port in England. The legacy is a magnificent waterfront location for urban regeneration. The creation of BBC's MediaCity:UK is the latest initiative in the docklands renaissance

Images courtesy of Peel Holdings

Right Peel Holdings ownership of the dock estates on both sides of the river have created the opportunity for potentially the most ambitious city planning in Liverpool and Birkenhead's history. Facing twin developments called Wirral Waters (right) and Liverpool Waters (far right) will create a waterside that will rival Sydney, Shanghai or Manhattan. The £10 billion developments will create tens of thousands of jobs and bring back to life the hundreds of acres of derelict docks on both sides of the river.

Images courtesy of Peel Holdings

anchor in Liverpool, including the Queen Mary II, the Queen Elizabeth II and the Grand Princess.

Whether it's turbines, new visitors looking to encounter Liverpool Capital of Culture for 2008 or container ships trading with North America, one corporate entity more than any other re-occurs as a constant as the future of the Mersey is considered: Peel Holdings.

With an asset base of more than £4.5 billion, Peel is fundamental to the future of the Mersey. The company owns the Trafford Centre, a major retail and leisure complex on the outskirts of Manchester; it operates the Mersey Docks, Clydeport and the Manchester Ship Canal; and it operates airports at Liverpool, Durham Tees Valley and Doncaster Sheffield.

In addition to the tidal power scheme and new container ship facility, on the Wirral Peninsula the company is planning 'Wirral Waters'. The level of aspiration for the scheme is high, with Peel planning a £4.5 billion

redevelopment of Birkenhead docks that will create a waterside destination to rival Sydney, New York and Shanghai. Covering a massive 18 million square feet, the scheme will include new employment areas, a major new retail and leisure quarter, not to mention 50 storey skyscrapers. The shorthand for the vision for some is a new 'Manhattan on the Mersey' and Peel estimates that it will create some 27,000 new jobs.

Wirral Waters is mirrored across the estuary in 'Liverpool Waters', this time a £5.5 billion development with a similar mix of skyscrapers, landscaping and in this case a monorail linking through to the (Peel-owned) Liverpool Airport. It is the biggest scheme of its kind to occur in the Northwest for more than a century and will include 25,000 apartments, four hotels, shops, bars, restaurants and marina facilities.

Peel's reach extends back along the Ship Canal to Salford and another development that will have national implications. The Ship Canal ends at

Pomona Docks where a footbridge connects through to Salford Quays (another regeneration success story where pioneering environmental techniques have been used to such good effect that the formerly polluted waters are in such a good state that they now play host to an annual triathlon).

Here Peel is building a new home for the BBC, called MediaCity:UK. More than just a new headquarters for the Corporation's sports, digital and Five Live output, MediaCity:UK will become Britain's first purpose built media city, based on a 200-acre site just outside the city centre of Manchester. Given the final go-ahead by the Government in January 2007, the BBC has confirmed the site as its chosen location and will be the catalyst for a major programme of development that will bring £1 billion into the economy over the next five years, will attract private investment of over £300m in the first phase, will create the space for 1,150 creative businesses and provide jobs for 15,500 people. It will take its place alongside the Lowry and Imperial War Museum North and will include a new iconic building on the waterfront for the BBC.

Some of the visions jar with each other. How can so much development take place as we begin a global battle to reduce our ecological footprint? Where does a deep sea container port fit in to the fight against climate change? How can the benefits of a new media industry or a new cultural renaissance be felt through every community, in each and every neighbourhood?

Thud, thud. The residents of North Wirral heard the shafts of Burbo Bank wind farm being pile driven into the sands of the Irish Sea day after day, after

day. Thud, thud. Along the beach at Crosby, 100 metre-long foundation poles have been set and then topped off with life-sized sculptures in man-shaped forms, Antony Gormley's Another Place. Thud, thud. A new arena is looming on the historic waterfront at Liverpool. Business is brisk at Liverpool John Lennon Airport. Stanlow is still making petrol, not hydrogen.

Great care will have to be taken to avoid the mistakes of the past in the name of truly sustainable development, but with a few caveats, perhaps, the future is looking good along the Mersey.

At its mouth of the Mersey, Liverpool stands square as a European Capital of Culture. From the Gormley sculptures that the good people of Crosby have fought to keep in the face of bureaucracy and petty-mindedness, to the endlessly pioneering Liverpool Biennial of Contemporary Art, the city seems to act as a factory of ideas regardless of powerplays or media speculation.

It must be something in the water.

The river courses with change and with dreams. It is an artery in every sense. But what of the people, of the local communities? If there were one challenge greater than any other in the Mersey's future it would be reaching through to the forgotten, the disenfranchised and the disillusioned. The Mersey tracks its course through some of England's most deprived communities and if new power, or new culture are to mean anything, they have to deliver social change, as well as a better environment.

ALONG THE BANKS

DAVID WARD

In my end is my beginning. New Brighton is where the Mersey stops and the sea starts and the firm wide sands that wrap round this top right-hand corner of the Wirral demand to be walked upon on a breezy, sun-filled day of late summer.

People amble, dogs run, oystercatchers dig. A black cat tip-toeing round the royal crest high on the sandstone walls of Fort Perch Rock eyes me snootily as I clamber down towards the breakwater that I have unilaterally decided marks the boundary between fresh and salt water lapping at my feet.

In cities, we usually look down on rivers from an embankment, a bridge. Here I am almost eye to eye with the Mersey. It's a new perspective, just one of many experienced in these ramblings. Things look different: a cargo boat at journey's end beating up the river; six wind turbines turning; Bootle docks waiting for trade. I just hang about with the wind in my hair and look east along sun-shimmering water to where Liverpool's two cathedrals and the Liver birds are silhouetted against a perfect sky.

Behind me is Perch Rock lighthouse, left high and dry at this morning's low tide; it has been here for 180 years, thirty of them in light-less retirement. The chunky fort nearby has seen little action and today offers no violence, only an 'Elvis Meets the Beatles Art and Memorabilia Exhibition'.

Once its ramparts bristled with ordnance but its active service has been both limited and erratic. As the First World War began, one of its guns fired a shot across the bow of a Norwegian ship which did not comply with a warning signal. The shot missed by miles, thumping into the beach at Crosby.

The fort's commander, a territorial officer and a dentist in real life, ordered his men to fire a second shot, which smacked into the bow of a liner innocently anchored in the river.

Enough of these Mersey-like meanderings. It's time to head upriver to Sainsbury's in Stockport. I used to do my shopping here but had no idea that the Mersey begins nearby and I was only dimly aware that a shopping centre called Merseyway must have something to do with the river.

So today I go in search of its source. Along Great Egerton Street, packed with cars looking for somewhere to park, and then left over a bridge, and left again to a kind of promontory marked by tired decorative iron work bearing a message whose meaning is clear despite the missing letters: 'Here ri ers Goyt & Tame becom Mersey flowing clear from Stockport to the sea.'

This is the confluence that makes the Mersey. It is a significant but far from beautiful spot. Supermarket trolleys mark the last yards of the Goyt; the Tame limps in under a utilitarian bridge bearing the M60. The two waters meet with little ceremony and are brutally bent by the motorway embankment round the back of Sainsbury's. The young river is then shoved out of sight and out of mind under a branch of Barclay's bank.

This is not how a mighty waterway should begin. So I head for the Peak District in search of the source of the Goyt and a rather more Wordsworthian experience. It is a soggy day of relentless rain driven by a warm west wind. I drive in and out of mist past the Cat and Fiddle pub on the Macclesfield to Buxton road (the most dangerous in Britain) and down to Derbyshire bridge, dump the car, pull on the cagoule and hat and search for the beginning among the heather.

Is it here? Or here? Over there? A kestrel is above my head, the air is full of the sound of gurgling and my feet are getting wet. I cross the moor, turn right on to a track and am deceived by more false watery starts. Eventually I am on the lane along which I arrived and see a peaty torrent. This must be the Goyt, but it seems more of a toddler here than a new-born. I risk a look at a map rapidly turning to pulp. Fool: the source is obviously on Axe Edge moor on the other side of the Cat and Fiddle road. I am too wet to care.

But later, on that sunny day on the strand at New Brighton, I peer at the wide river and wonder if the Pennine water I saw that rainy day in the Goyt valley has yet passed this way. Then I start thinking about fish. We know that salmon have been exploring the cleaned-up Mersey in recent years but in 2005 three young fish were found in the Goyt, proof that salmon have travelled from the Irish Sea to the Cheshire uplands to breed.

It's not just salmon that have noticed the difference. On the sands at the mouth of the Mersey, anglers wait patiently by rods fixed on tripods. "The river is much cleaner now," explains one. "We're fishing for fluke today. But in six weeks the cod will be coming past here."

Cod? In the Mersey? Quite true, says Ian McKay, of Sefton Sea Anglers. "Cod are caught as far up as Otterspool and the only reason they have not been caught further up the river is that we haven't fished there. The cod come in October or November and stay until February or March."

I'm learning fast. And my whole attitude to the river is changing as my explorations continue. I've shot across the Mersey at hair-raising speeds on an inshore rescue boat; I've listened to the Royal Liverpool Philharmonic play the finale of Tchaikovsky's fourth symphony in the Kingsway tunnel far below the river bed; and at dusk, on a wondrously still spring day, I steered a Mersey ferry past the Pier Head at the end of a long journey down the Manchester Ship Canal from Trafford.

But most of the time I'm in a car and the Mersey gets in my way. I regularly cross it at the end of the M56, or over Thelwall Viaduct or the stately Runcorn Bridge. But now I'm travelling along it, going mainly with the flow, peering at maps to find byways to its banks, flitting from the intensely urban to the sweetly bucolic and back again.

One day begins with a busy highway, the newish section of the A57 that bypasses Cadishead on its way to Irlam. I dodge the road near a high railway bridge (graffiti signed by Liam and Chris) to find where the river joins and is swallowed by the ship canal. And there it is, the

Mersey's mucky white water dropping down a 10ft weir clogged with junk and branches. Nearby are tired bushes and a lone swan. Any Goyt-bound salmon who swims this way must be very determined.

Back in the car, I head west past sewage farms, factories, oil tanks and cement plants and eventually flat fields to a junction with the M6.

A path leads over a stile to the river, which after three miles or so, has abandoned the ship canal and gone its own way towards Warrington. The aim is to reach that parting of the ways but first I turn right and almost immediately spot a cormorant, who shoves off as soon as he sees me.

I walk on until I am under the Thelwall Viaduct, or more correctly, viaducts. The new one (built to permit four lanes heading north and south) opened in the nineties at 1.15 in the morning: I know – I was there; the old one creaks and grumbles ominously. The racket under the bridges is awful and contrasts with the slow, silent amble of the river. It's all a bit depressing.

So I turn round, and head east following the line of the Mersey Way path until the sound of the traffic fades and I can hear the blackbirds singing and my wet trainers swishing through the long grass. I can also hear guns. In the middle of a field, two men are staging a private clay pigeon shoot. They cease fire as I approach, resisting the temptation to take a pot shot at a larger, slower moving target. "The change in the river has been amazing in the last 10-15 years," says one. "You saw the cormorant? Where the fish are, that's where the cormorants will be. There are salmon here now. Look, there's a rise there in the water. And another."

I walk on, thinking of those salmon holding their breath as they prepare to dart up the ship canal and into the Mersey's upper reaches. My path leads on through beech woods and the Mersey Way turns away from the river. But I carry straight on, climb a gate and enter a field. The map tells me I am trespassing but I want to find that junction of river and ship canal. Half a mile from the meeting point and opposite a place called

Butchersfield I am stopped in my tracks by a barbed wire fence near a willow and a fallen tree covered with a delicate pink and white flower.

A scamper through the flora books suggests that this is Indian (or Himalayan) balsam, otherwise known, according to Richard Mabey, as policeman's helmet, stinky pops, jumping jacks, bee-bums, poor man's orchid – and Mersey weed. It was introduced from the Himalayas in 1839, has no fear of industrial pollution and loves colonising river banks by firing off its seeds like a machine gun and sending them floating on the water. I didn't sniff it but someone quoted by Mabey says it has "a pervasive evening scent reminiscent of Jeyes fluid".

I stumble on it almost everywhere I walk. On the Mersey's most boring stretch, where the river is subjugated by thuggish flood defences from Didsbury westwards, it is one of the few flowers to cheer you up on a plod along the towpath.

On another day, I go in search of Thelwall because WE Palmer, whose book on the Mersey was published in 1944, said he couldn't find it. Perhaps he didn't look very hard. There it is on the south bank of the ship canal, near the Pickering Arms which proclaims: "In the year 920, King Edward the Elder founded a city here and called it Thelwall."

My plan is to take the Thelwall passenger ferry across the canal and explore the no man's land between its northern bank and the Mersey's Warrington loops. I walk down Ferry Lane to the ferryman's house in a well-manicured glade but I have missed the boat. So I drive round to Victoria Park in Warrington to search for Howley Weir, at the Mersey's tidal limit. An unlovely path leads me to a surprise, a beautiful cast iron and timber suspension footbridge, far more elegant than it need be to carry joggers and dog walkers across the river. It's built-in bounce gives a sensation of walking on air. On the other side, a track leads past small factories, dumped plastic bags and anglers hoping for eels, bream and roach to the disused Howley lock, where an overgrown sycamore plunges almost into the water.

I push on westwards out of Warrington, past Widnes and take the minor road through Hale Bank and then Hale to Hale Head and its grubby white lighthouse overlooking Dungeon Banks and the other great expanses of mud and sand where the river opens up to a width of about one and a half miles. The light is eerie and misty and the opposite bank has been reduced to a mere possibility; it's a like a Lowry sea-meets-sky picture.

The mud is grey, resembling an irregularly-patterned woollen rug, and is covered with birds taking inter-tidal afternoon tea. The Mersey estuary, according to the Royal Society for the Protection of Birds, supports more than 100,000 ducks and waders (half of them dunlin) and experts suggest that one cubic metre of Mersey mud contains enough worms and insects to match the calorie content of 16 Mars bars.

I have brought my binoculars but I am hopeless at identifying birds. So I take on trust the information board's claim that through the mist I can see dunlin, wigeon, teal, shelduck, bar-tailed godwit and redshank. But even I know the curlew's cry. And that big bird perched on a rocky outcrop is a heron and that other thing in the sky is an easyJet aircraft on approach to John Lennon Airport.

I follow in its slipstream for a couple of miles, with the light ever changing, and then turn back, almost stumbling over what I am pretty sure was a merlin preparing for take-off. Reluctant to leave, I go round to Hale Cliff, another point of access to the river and its mudflats. Here there is a scruffy car park, where people gather at the back of the runway to spot hair-parting planes rather than birds.

This is something I have noticed frequently in this journey. People are drawn to points of arrival and departure: here at an international airport; at New Brighton, where boats come and go; at Jackson's Boat Inn by an ancient crossing of the Mersey on the edge of Sale Water Park; but most of all at Eastham on the Wirral.

The seven-mile ferry link between Eastham and Liverpool is mentioned 143 in the Domesday Book and in the 18th century was a regular stage in the trip from Chester to Liverpool. By the time a new iron pier and floating landing stage were added in 1874, ferries were running every half hour because Eastham had become the perfect place for a day trip.

Pleasure gardens developed in the mid 19th century boasted a hotel, open air stage, ballroom, pavilion, boating lake, water chute and loop-the-loop, a rickety precursor of the roller coaster. There was also a zoological garden with tropical birds, seals, bears (polar, black, brown and silver), lions, leopards, zebras, elks, camels, ocelots, cassowaries and monkeys.

Charles Blondin, the great aerialist, came here once and hired a Bromborough lad and pushed him along a tightrope in a wheelbarrow but does not appear to have attempted a high-wire crossing of the Mersey.

Pearl, Ruby and Sapphire, the last of the paddle steamer ferries, stopped running in 1929 and the iron pier was demolished six years later. But go to Eastham country park on a pleasant day and you will still find people loitering by the hotel and glancing to the river, as if waiting for the ferry to return, bringing hundreds of ghostly Scousers to revive memories of exotic animals and a fearless, sure-footed Frenchman.

If my beginning was at the Mersey's end, my end will not be at the river's beginning, whether that is in a battered corner of Stockport or in the rain-swollen Goyt on Axe Edge moor. This journey finishes somewhere not quite in the middle, but nearer the mouth than the source.

Spike Island, just by the Runcorn Bridge at Widnes, was to sulphuric acid what Eastham was to pleasure. The chemical industry and its muddle of railway lines prospered for not much more than 50 years.

From the 1930s, Spike Island was a derelict, polluted dump for 40 years until Halton Council and Cheshire County Council reclaimed it, turning it into a magical Mersey-side green and tranquil space where families feed swans and men mess about with boats.

A small fleet is moored in the middle of the broad Sankey canal, with lock access to the Mersey down river from the great bulk of Fiddler's Ferry power station. Miranda II, Life O'Reilly and Nora Batty are safely parked but Rita and Sangar are missing. "They're out in the Med now, Portugal I think," says Stephen Lawson from Speke. "That one – Laura Gem – is just back from the Isle of Man."

"There are handy fellas here – some can do woodwork, others fibre glass or welding. We all help each other. I've just re-fibre glassed my own boat but I haven't been anywhere yet. I save up, do a little bit and then do a bit more. It's just a hobby. It's better than sitting in the house."

Spike Island, it emerges, is like an allotment, with boats instead of rhubarb; a self-sufficient contented community. It's a tricky place to find – take the wrong turn off the big bridge and you will never find your way. But I'm here now, the afternoon sun is still warm and here's a bench. I'm going to sit on it and watch the Mersey glide by.

MERSEY ROAD

COLIN McPHERSON

The brief was straightforward: to photograph the river Mersey, from source to sea. Interpreting such a project would be more difficult. How do you capture the essence of a waterway that begins as a trickle high in the Peak District and empties out into Liverpool Bay – encompassing rural beauty, industrial decay, regeneration and economic wealth? That passes major towns and cities and is a visual testament to the region's history. That twists through undiscovered and forgotten backwaters. And that touches peoples' lives and provides employment and enjoyment for many.

The Mersey revealed so many secrets and surprises at every turn that it proved easy to photograph. Over the course of a year, I spent so long in the river's company that I discovered how a modern river works. It provides work for some, recreation for others and shapes the environment around it. It is an inspiration for artists and rich historical resource for future generations.

I was captivated by the form and function of the river; an environment shaped by the human hand that I photographed without people. I looked for the extremes of night and day, hot and cold, light and dark. And all the while the Mersey was a good companion to me. In the end, the river, as it has for so many people, became my friend.

Left Mersey Road, Runcorn.

Shooter's Clough, Goyt Valley.

Errwood Reservoir,
Goyt Valley.

149

Confluence of the rivers Tame and Goyt, Stockport.

Stockport Viaduct.

Disused railway
viaduct, Heaton
Mersey.

Caravan site,
Northenden.

The Lowry, Salford Quays.

Offices, Salford Quays.

Barton Bridge and
Aqueduct.

Barton Bridge and
Aqueduct.

The Manchester Ship
Canal and Thelwall
Viaduct.

The Mersey at
Woolston Weir.

Woolston Nature
Reserve.

The Manchester Ship
Canal at Thelwall.

Industrial estate,
Latchford Locks.

The Mersey at
Warrington.

Howley Bridge,
Warrington.

Fiddler's Ferry power
station, from Penketh.

Fiddler's Ferry power station from Wigg Island.

The Silver Jubilee
Bridge, from Runcorn.

The Silver Jubilee Bridge,
from Wigg Island.

Factory, West Bank,
Widnes.

Chemical works,
Weston, Runcorn.

Stanlow Oil Refinery,
from Speke.

Mudflats, Speke.

Road to oil refinery, Elton.

Arterial road in a new
industrial estate, Speke.

175

Ince Marshes, from
Elton.

Stanlow Oil Refinery,
from Elton.

Football pitches, New Ferry.

Disused business,
Dock Road, Liverpool.

Greenland Street
during the Liverpool
Biennial.

Landing stage,
Birkenhead.

Statue of immigrant family, Albert Dock, Liverpool.

Ferry crossing the Mersey to Seacombe, Wirral.

The Liver Building and
new landing stages,
Pier Head, Liverpool.

185

Queensway tunnel
building, Birkenhead.

Passenger foot tunnel,
James Street station,
Liverpool.

The Paradise project under construction, Liverpool.

West Float, Wallasey.

Stanley Road,
Liverpool.

Loading a container
ship, Seaforth Docks.

Perch Rock lighthouse,
New Brighton.

King's Parade, New Brighton.

195

Bright Spot Amusement
Park, New Brighton.

Lifeguard station, New Brighton.

A statue from Antony Gormley's Another Place, Crosby beach.

Crosby beach.

A statue from Antony Gormley's Another Place, Crosby beach.

Ainsdale Nature
Reserve, Formby.

Formby.

CONTRIBUTORS

Ian Wray is chief planner with the Northwest Regional Development Agency. He studied planning at University College London, and geography at the University of Newcastle upon Tyne. He has contributed to the Architects Journal, Management Today, the Guardian and the Times. Born in Manchester, he lives in Birkenhead, just within sight (and very occasionally sound) of the Mersey.

Edwin Colyer is a writer. He has contributed to local and national publications ranging from the Financial Times to the Northwest Enquirer. His particular areas of interest include science, technology, and the environment. Edwin also writes regularly on topical business issues, especially marketing and branding. He enjoys living close to Rusholme's 'curry mile', has two small children, and a canoe in his garden shed.

John Belchem is professor of history at the University of Liverpool. Author of *Merseypride: Essays in Liverpool Exceptionalism*, he is also the editor of *Liverpool 800: Culture, Character and History*, commissioned by the City Council and the University of Liverpool to mark the 800th anniversary in 2007.

Peter de Figueiredo is an architect and architectural historian working for English Heritage. He gives advice on major historic sites and monuments in the north-west region. He is the author of several books and articles on architecture and conservation.

Kate Fox wrote the 'Mersey People' interviews and is new media co-ordinator at the Mersey Basin Campaign. She studied English at the University of Nottingham before returning to the Northwest to work in the publishing industry. She writes regularly for SourceNW magazine. Born in Manchester, Kate lives close to the banks of the Mersey in Chorlton-cum-Hardy, and is the proud co-owner of a successful non-league football club.

Deborah Mulhearn is a journalist and writer. She has worked for publications as diverse as the Architects Journal and the Liverpool Echo. She lives in Liverpool but has been known to cross the Mersey occasionally.

Anthony H Wilson was a broadcast journalist and regeneration consultant. He founded the famous Hacienda night club (now closed) and was one of the five co-founders of Factory records – a label that set the trend not only in music, but also by pioneering a minimalist style of graphic and interior design. Factory's stark northern industrial chic was the counterpoint to London, and helped turn Manchester into (arguably) the music and night club capital of the world. Sadly, he died during the preparation of this book.

Michael Taylor is editorial director of Insider Media and edits North West Business Insider. He was born in Lancaster and educated at Lancaster Royal Grammar School and the University of Manchester and completed his journalism training in London. He has written for a wide range of business magazines and contributed to books on business, careers and industry. He lives in Marple, close to the source of the Mersey, with his wife Rachel and their five sons.

Chris Baines is an environmental campaigner and adviser to government and major companies. He is a writer and broadcaster, best known for championing urban wildlife since the late 1970s. He is a member of the Expert Panel of the Heritage Lottery Fund and also advises the Big Lottery. He is a national Vice President of the Royal Society of Wildlife Trusts and the Countryside Management Association, President of the Urban Wildlife Network and the Thames Estuary Partnership, and a Trustee of the Waterways Trust.

Paul Unger is a journalist based in Liverpool. Formerly business editor of the Liverpool Daily Post, he covers the Northwest's commercial property and regeneration industries for national business magazines.

Steve Connor is co-founder and chief executive officer of Creative Concern. His recent projects have included strategic communications for Manchester City Council, the Forestry Commission, Mersey Waterfront, Northwest Regional Development Agency and Manchester Enterprises. He is chair of the Northwest's Regional Forestry Framework, a board member of Envirolink Northwest and on the advisory board of Salford University's Centre for Sustainable Urban and Regional Futures. He lives in the People's Republic of Chorlton with his partner Anne and their daughter Madeleine.

David Ward grew up in London and studied English at the University of London. His first job in journalism was in Northumberland and, following spells on regional newspapers, he joined the Guardian in Manchester in 1974. He is now one of the paper's two Manchester-based northern correspondents.

Colin McPherson is a photojournalist who regularly covers news and features for the print media both at home and abroad. He also works on long-term projects and exhibits his work widely. Colin moved from his native Scotland to the Wirral four years ago and is a contributing editorial photographer with Corbis.

Note: all the contributors are expressing personal views, which are not necessarily those of their employers, nor of the Mersey Basin Campaign.

INDEX

A

Abney Hall 30
African chant 101
Albert Dock 10, 12, *13*, 41, 69, 70, *80*, 81,
106, 124, *126*, 127, *183*
Alexander, Brian 127
Arkwright, Richard 24, 25
Amhairgain 9
Ashanti dance 101
Atherton, James 45

B

Baco-Liner 110
Bank Quay transporter bridge 33, 89
Barlow Hall 33
Batey, Peter 127
BBC MediaCity: UK 137
BB King 102
Berry, Chuck 96, 98
Bibby Line 106
Birkenhead 29, 45, 49, 81, *85*, 86, 105, 114,
117, *134*, *182*, *186*, *187*
Birkenhead Docks 45, 134
Birkenhead Park 117
Blondin, Charles 144
Blues 10, 11, 98, 100-102
Bolton and Watt 21
Bottleneck 102
Bridgewater Canal 21, 34, 37, 93
Brindley Centre 37
Brindley, James 93
Britannia Railway Bridge, Runcorn 86
Bromborough Pool 38
Bronowski, Dr 27
Bronze Age 16
Brookes, slave ship *100*, 101
Bryson, Bill 123
Burbo Bank *130*, 131, 137

C

Cadbury 110

Cargills 106
Carthage 16
Celtic Brittany 16
Central Park, New York 17
Charleston 100, 110
Chesshyre, Sir John 33
Chester 9, 15, 16, 21, 33, 37, 93, 144
Clapton, Eric 101
Climate change 17, 131, 132, 137
Cockles 117, 118
Containers *102*, 105, *108*, 109, 110, *133*,
134, 137, *193*
Control of Pollution Act, 1974 121, 122
Cornovii 16
Country music 11
Cunard Yanks 11
Curlews 78, 113, 118, 143,

D

DDT 114
Deceangeli 16
Defoe, Daniel 11, 12, 81
Delph wool scribbling mill 29
Diddley, Bo 98
Donbavand, Thomas 22
Duke of Westminster 12
Dwek, Joe 127

E

Eastham 37, 38, 81, 82, 95, 143, 144, *179*
Ellesmere Port 37, 38, 81, 127, *141*
Ellesmere Port (National Waterways Museum)
37, *40*
Endocrine disrupters 113
Environment Agency 113, 128
Estuary 9, 15, 37, 66, 78, 81, 95, 98, 113,
117, 118, 121, 131, 134, 143
Ethelfleda, Queen 16
European Metals Recycling 106
European structural funds 123

F

Fiddler's Ferry *32*, 33, 81, 82, 144, *166*, *167*
Fort Perch Rock *44*, 45, 139
Freeport 106, 109

G

Garden festivals *124*, *125*, 127
Gates, Bill 12
Glester, John 128
Gormley, Antony 137, *198*, *201*
Goyt 29, 95, 102, 113, 139, 140, 144, *148*,
149, *150*
Griffiths, Dr David 15-17
Groundwork Trust 114

H

Hale *36*, 37, 81, 143
Hale duck decoy 37
Hale Ford 81
Hale Point 37
Halton Castle *32*, 33
Hamilton Square 45
Hamp, Johnny 98
Hartley, Jesse 41, 124
Heinz 110
Heseltine, Michael 11, 41, 62, *63*, 121-124,
127, 128
Hooton Park 38
Hough End Hall 33
Howley Weir 113, 128, 143
Hume, Rev. Abraham 15, 17

I

Imperial War Museum North *11*, 137
Ince Manor 37
Ineos 29, *91*
Iron Age 16

J

Jenkin, Patrick 122, 123
Joseph Crosfield & Sons 22, *24*, 25, 33, 89

K

King, Tom 122
Kingham, Norman 45
Kingsway Tunnel 140
Knot *115*, 118
Knowsley Wildflower Centre 114

L

Laird, William 45
Lake Vyrnwy 81
Landlife 114
Land reclamation 114
Lever, WH, First Viscount Leverhulme 41
Libeskind, Daniel 11
Liverpool
    Capital of Culture 2008 41, 134, 137
    Cavern 98
    City centre 10, 12, 86, 106
    Cruise liner facility 133
    Decline 85, 121
    First wet dock 10
    John Lennon Airport 38, 128, 137, 143
    Liverpool Biennial of Contemporary Art 137
    Liverpool Waters 134, *135*
    Pier Head *13*, 41, 58, 69, 70, 105, 106,
    140, *185*
    School of Tropical Medicine 12
    World Heritage Site 10, 41, 43, *44*, 57
Lowland bogs 113
Lugworms 117, 118

M

Manchester Ship Canal *10*, *11*, 30, 33, 37,
38, 66, 81, 82, 85, 86, 89, 90, *91*, 93, 95,
105, 113, 117, 121, 127, 131, 134, 140,
141, *158*, *161*
Mausoleum of Hallicarnassos 45
McCartney, Michael 98
McCartney, Paul 97
Meols 9, *13*, 15-19
Mersey Barrage 86

Mersey Basin Campaign 127, 128
Mersey Docks and Harbour Company 105, 109, 128, 133
Mersey-Irwell Navigation 21
Mersey Road Tunnel 85
Mersey Way 140
Merseyside Development Corporation 124
Merseyside Task Force 121
Middleton, John ('Childe of Hale') 37
Militant Tendency 122
Mott, Sir Basil 85

N
National Waterways Museum 37, *40*
Norse Merchant Ferries 105
North West Water Authority 122, 123, 127
Norton Priory 33, 34

O
Objective One 128
Old English 9, 81
Oldknow, Samuel 95, 96
Orchids 114, *115*, 143
Oystercatcher 115, 118, *119*, 139

P
Paxton, Joseph 45
Peak Forest Canal *94*, 96
Peel Holdings 12, 45, 127, 128, 131, *132*, 133, *134*
Perch Rock Lighthouse 45, *104*, 139, *194*
Philpott, Dr Rob 15-19
Pollution 27, 34, 54, 73, 113, 114, 118, 121, 122, 128, 143
Port Sunlight 38, 41
Post-Panamax 110, *133*
Prescott, John 128
Presley, Elvis 11, 98, 138
Priestley, Joseph 25, 26
Princes Dock 105, *120*
Privatisation 123, 127, 128

Pugin, Augustus Welby 30
Pugin, Edward Welby 30
Pyramid office building 30, *31*

Q
Quarry Bank Mill 29

R
Ramsar convention 118
Raw sewage outfalls 121, 122
Rio Pongas 100
River St Paul 100
RMS Tayleur 26
Roman Lakes 95
Rowse, Herbert 86
Rubie's Masquerade Company 109
Runcorn 9, 21, *32*, 34, *35*, 37, 81, 82, 86, 89, 121, 137, 140, 144, *146*, *168*, *171*
Runcorn (Silver Jubilee) Bridge *10*, 37, *35*, 81, 82, 87, 89, 140, 144, *168*, *169*
Runcorn New Town 37
Rylands Brothers 22

S
St Christopher statue 34
St Elphin, Warrington 33
Sail cloth 22
Sale Water Park 90, 143
Salford Quays *11*, 127, 137, *154*, *155*
Salmon 9, 11, 22, 113, *116*, 140
Sandon Dock 69, 106, 123, 124
Sankey Valley 117
Scrap metal 105, 106, *109*
Seacombe Ferry 82
Seaforth Dock 8, *104*, 106, 133, *142*, *193*
Sefton Park *115*
Sewage 73, 106, 113, 117, 121, 122, 123, 140
Sex Pistols 98, 100
Shelduck 117, 118, 143
Slave trade 10, *99*, *100*, 101, 102

Sorenson, Eric 121
Special Protection Area 118
Speke Hall 38, 39
Spike Island 37, 144, *145*
Stanley Dock 41, 106
Stanlow 37, 38, 65, 113, *116*, 131, 137, *172*, *177*
Stanlow Abbey 37
Staircase House 30
Stockport 10, 29, 30, *31*, 81, 92, 93, 95, 139, 144, *150*, *151*
Straddle carriers 110
Stubs, Peter 24, 25
Swordfish 113

T
Tate and Lyle 106
Tate Liverpool art gallery 124, 127
Tavare, John 127
Taylor, John Edward 33
Telford, Thomas 37, 38
Thatcher, Margaret 62, 121, 123, 127
Thelwall 143, *161*
Thelwall Eyes 82, *83*
Thelwall Viaduct 33, 82, 90, 140, 143, *158*
Thornton-le-Moors 37
Tidal fence 131
Tidal power 131, 134
Tides 15, 81, 117
Tobacco Warehouse 41
Townsend, Pete 101
Toxteth riots 121
Trent and Mersey Canal 34

U
UNESCO World Heritage Site 10
United Utilities 69, 78, 106, 127, 128

V
Vikings 16

W
Waders 118, 143
Wallasey Town Hall 45
Walton, Peter 121
Warburton, Old St Werburgh's Church 33
Warrington 9, 20-27, 29, 33, 41, 78, 82, 85, 86, 88, 89, 95, 113, 114, 121, 128, 140, 143, 163, *164*, *165*
Warrington Circulating Library 26
Warrington Dissenters' Academy 23, 25, 26, 27
Water quality 70, 78, *116*, 121, 127, 128
Watkin, Sir Edward 33
Watts, Sir James 30
Weaver Navigation 21
Wellington Wheel 95
Widnes 34, 35, 37, 78, 81, 82, 87, 114, 121, 143, 144, *145*, *170*
Wilderspool 21
Wirral Waters 45, *134*
Whittaker, John 127
Work song 101, 102
Worthington, Thomas 33